THE CALL
TO HOLINESS

Embracing a Fully Christian Life

THE CALL
TO HOLINESS

❖

Embracing a Fully Christian Life

Richard M. Gula, S.S.

PAULIST PRESS
New York/Mahwah, N.J.

The scripture quotations contained herein are from the New Revised Standard Version Bible, copyright © 1989 by the Division of Christian Education of the National Council of the Churches of Christ in the U.S.A. and are used by permission. All rights reserved.

Cover design by Cindy Dunne
Book design by Lynn Else

Copyright © 2003 by Richard M. Gula

Library of Congress Cataloging-in-Publication Data

Gula, Richard M.
    The call to holiness : embracing a fully Christian Life / Richard M. Gula.
        p. cm.
    Includes bibliographical references.
    ISBN 0-8091-4130-2
    1. Christian ethics—Catholic authors. 2. Christian life—Catholic authors.
3. Spirituality—Catholic Church. 4. Holiness—Catholic Church. I. Title.
    BJ1249 .G815 2003
    241—dc21

                                                                2002156335

Published by Paulist Press
997 Macarthur Boulevard
Mahwah, New Jersey 07430

www.paulistpress.com

Printed and bound in the United States of America

Contents

✤

Introduction

❀

Spirituality is in. Ever since the cultural revolution of the '60s, spirituality has had a grip on the imagination of believers and non-believers alike. The interest in spirituality has been of two kinds: either deeply individualistic, allied with a cult of inwardness and personal growth, or other-directed, seeking to integrate soul and society, the sanctuary and the street, Sunday's worship and Monday's work. This book participates in the movement toward integration.

The hunger for the spiritual is evident everywhere. Retreat houses are full. Courses with "spirituality" in the title are oversubscribed. Conferences on spiritual practices and traditions fill up quickly, whether they are on Eastern meditation, Native American spiritualities, goddess rituals, Twelve Step programs, New Age techniques for healing or self-improvement, or classic Western monasticism. Complaints about emptiness and meaninglessness or yearnings for personal fulfillment equally reflect cravings of the soul. The soul is searching for sustenance. In fact, I would not be surprised if you picked up this book, at least to skim it, in the hope that it might have some spiritual nourishment to feed your soul.

1

THE CALL TO HOLINESS

The hunger of the soul has made spirituality a new cottage industry for book sellers and the media giants. The shelves of our large bookstores fill with new titles weekly to include everything from memoirs of personal journeys in faith, to new translations of classical mysticism, to books on managing the corporation's "soul," to New Age healing, to the occult. Such an intense interest is baffling, for it is not clear what people are talking about when they refer to "spirituality." Just look at the many different kinds of books shelved in the bookstore under "Spirituality." Do all of them really belong together?

If we are not careful, we can be deceived by the way spirituality is marketed as a sphere in its own right or as a product for the "inner life" and self-development. In either instance spirituality is not being connected to the way we live out the daily responsibilities of our lives. Just as it has become popular for some to separate spirituality and religion (as in the expression, "I'm spiritual but not religious!"), so it can seem that spirituality is not necessary for morality either. This book will focus on the relation of spirituality and morality in the light of faith.

Stimulus for this book comes from two sources. One is the positive reception of my last book from Paulist Press, *The Good Life*. That book tried to provide a vision of what life might look like when spirituality and morality converge. One of the criticisms I received about that book is that it failed to explain the presuppositions that would make its vision credible. This book tries to respond to that. So, in that sense, this book is volume 1 with *The Good Life* being volume 2.

The other stimulus comes from my experiences as a consultant in clinical ethics for hospitals, where I listen to people trying to explain their moral disagreements. The following, for example, is a case in medical ethics that typifies how moral dilemmas entail spiritual issues that help to create a moral impasse. T.K. has just turned seventy-five. He was a strong patriarchal figure whose word was law. He raised one son, and his wife never had to work outside the home. He lived a vigorous life and, since retirement, still liked to hike once a week and play with his three grandchildren. T.K. has been diagnosed with a form of pneumonia that is resistant to treatment. Gradually his lungs and heart have become seriously compromised, and he shows signs of increasing deterioration after each period on the respirator. Should he be resuscitated if his heart stops? Should he be placed on a respirator again if his lungs deteriorate further? In the course of discussing this case, three positions emerged that stood in conflict with one another. One was to use whatever intervention was necessary to keep T.K. alive, since he was a fighter throughout his life and expressed a determined will to overcome his illness. The second was to provide comfort care only in order to keep him free of pain until he died, since nothing more could be done to change his condition. The third was to induce death right away in order to put an end to everyone's suffering, his own and his family's.

Those who argued strictly from principles wanted to respect T.K.'s autonomy and prolong his life at any cost. They saw that keeping him alive would honor his wishes, show the respect that reverencing life requires, and avoid the illegal act of euthanasia.

Those who argued from a mix of principles and consequences wanted to provide comfort care only since it honored the principle "Do no harm" by not aggressively intervening, and it considered the consequences for T.K. and the family of prolonging the dying process. The strict consequentialists argued for inducing death, since it produced the best results for everyone by ending prolonged suffering and by avoiding mounting medical bills.

In the course of discussing this case, it became evident that people were at an impasse not just because they differed on moral methods of argument (principles versus consequences), but because they were divided on deeper matters of meaning (Why are we here? and, How much control do we need to live a meaningful life?), beliefs (How free are we? and, Does our freedom include the taking of life?), loyalties (Does loyalty mean that we always have to do what another asks of us?), and values (What makes life worth living? and, Is living in a seriously compromised condition that makes it impossible to enjoy pleasures in life the kind of life one must sustain at all costs?). These are all ways that one's spirituality influences one's morality. Judging the benefits and burdens of each option in this case is a spiritual exercise yielding a practical moral judgment. Yet the spiritual dimensions of a case like this seldom get named in the so-called moral deliberations. This book hopes to show that the moral life needs spirituality's orientation, and spirituality needs morality's application. Spirituality is the wider frame of meaning and awareness within which the moral life of character, choice, and action operate. In actual living, spiritual and moral concerns are interconnected, though we seldom attend to their connection.

Introduction

The second half of the twentieth century has left us with some heartening developments in the conversation between theological disciplines. This book participates in that dialogue by trying to show that Christian faith does indeed form and guide the moral life. It tries to help committed Christians in this pluralistic society make sense of their moral lives in light of Christian faith and their spiritual longing. The explicit recognition of the universal call to holiness by Vatican II (*LG* #39–41) has helped break down a two-tiered view of Christian life that put professional religious persons on a higher plane than the laity. If everyone is called to attain union with God, then spirituality and the morality of everyday life ought to be interrelated ways of developing one's relationship with God.

My hope for you is that when you finish this book you will be able to appreciate the fundamental conviction that inspired it: *Spirituality without morality is disembodied; morality without spirituality is rootless.* Our moral life arises out of our spirituality to become its public face. What we do to nurture our spirituality through spiritual practices can and ought to have an effect on our moral practices—on the kind of person we become, the way we make our choices, the habits we form, the priorities we set, and the way we ultimately live our lives. In turn, the way we live morally can and ought to feed our soul through the friends we keep, the communities we participate in, the ideals we aspire to, the attitudes and habits we nurture, the image we have of ourselves, and the values we strive to realize by the actions we do. In the end, I hope you will see that spirituality and morality converge when we consider life as a whole rather than simply focus on individual actions in the moral life or devotional practices in the spiritual life.

This book is divided into three parts. Part I: Tracing the Connections clarifies the key concepts of spirituality and morality and then explores historically what contributed to their separation. By looking back over where we have been, it will try to show that how we conceive the relationship between spirituality and morality depends on how we understand the nature and scope of moral theology and spirituality themselves. Part II: Uncovering the Foundations examines how our notions of being human and of our experiencing God connect spirituality and morality. Part III: Practicing the Faith explores the relation of prayer and eucharistic worship to the moral life and three aspects of our life in the Spirit—conversion, discipleship, and discernment.

I owe a great debt of thanks to many people who have helped me to focus and refine the position presented here. I am grateful to my students at the Graduate Theological Union in my seminar on "Ethics and Spirituality," where I first began to explore the ideas developed here. A special word of thanks goes to my colleague and collaborator in that course, Professor Martha Ellen Stortz of the Pacific Lutheran Theological Seminary in Berkeley. She and I have had many conversations about these ideas. She read each chapter as it was written and gave helpful feedback and needed encouragement along the way. I am indebted to my Sulpician community and the Franciscan School of Theology, who supported me on a sabbatical leave to begin work on this project. The faculty of the Franciscan School of Theology subsequently made very helpful observations that contributed to refining some of this material when I presented it to them during a faculty colloquium after my sabbatical.

I got many other people involved in reading all or part of this material as I was writing it. I can't thank them all, but I want to single out my Sulpician colleagues, Frs. Philip S. Keane, S.S., and James P. Oberle, S.S., who, along with Frs. Ronald Chochol and Richard C. Sparks, C.S.P., did a close reading that led to further refinements of the text. I am also grateful to the comments of Mrs. Marilyn Neri, who read the manuscript with the interest of the adult audience for whom it is intended. Fr. Stephen C. Rowan, of the Archdiocese of Seattle, patiently read the final manuscript and offered suggestions to make it more readable. The roll call of others who deserve credit can go on. They are more than I can name, but blame none of them for anything you find here.

PART I

❖

Tracing the Connections

1.

What Are We Talking About?

❖

The terms *spirituality* and *morality* resist easy definition. No universal agreement exists about their meaning, and the boundaries of their relationship are difficult to determine. Yet any attempt to bring spirituality and morality into creative relationship with one another requires that we settle on some features that help us to name the range of interest of each and to distinguish one area of concern from the other. This chapter tries to do that.

Spirituality

Spirituality has become a buzzword. It is used in religious circles for sure, just as one might expect. But it also appears frequently and unexpectedly in the corporate world in discussions about renewing organizations that are falling apart, or "losing their soul." It is also used to describe New Age practices, Twelve Step programs, holistic living, therapeutic strategies, and social reform movements. Spirituality is also used to refer to practices for developing the interior life such as prayer, retreats, and spiritual direction. Spirituality indeed covers a wide range of interests.

THE CALL TO HOLINESS

Although definitions of *spirituality* are elusive, we use the term all the time as though its meaning were obvious. What do you associate with "spirituality," or what do you think of when you name someone as "spiritual," or when you want to improve your "spiritual life"? Just what are we talking about when we talk about spirituality? Compare your connotations with the ones represented in the following models.

From the time he was thirteen, the "Pillar Saint," Simeon Stylites (390–459), devoted his life to prayer, fasting, and other austerities, including physical punishment of his body, in ways that even exceeded the monastic practices of his time. In fact, he left the monastery to seek stricter austerity and seclusion by living on a small platform on top of a pillar (thus the nickname, "Pillar Saint"). As a solitary ascetic, he adopted body-denying disciplines in order to curb his passions so that he could be totally open to God. He fasted completely every Lent for twenty-six years. He believed that continual prayer, fasting, humiliation, and patient suffering were the road to eternal happiness and that the solitary life was the best opportunity to practice the virtues.[1] Simeon Stylites reflects one expression of the ascetical model of spirituality, and an extreme version at that. His asceticism conjures images of monastic celibates, wan and emaciated with eyes gazing heavenward. This way is optional. It is for those few who have a particular bent for it, since it demands striving for perfection through rigorous ascetical practices exceeding the scope and intensity of ordinary believers.

While Simeon's self-denial may be extreme, self-denial is a characteristic feature of this approach to spirituality. In its best form, ascetical self-denial fosters a simplicity of life, a concentration on God, and growth in love. We only need to think of how Francis of Assisi has fascinated so many and attracted such a following over the centuries with his way of integrating ascetical simplicity with generous service.

On the debit side, the ascetical model of spirituality risks opposing matter and spirit, with the spiritual realm being considered a separate sphere of life that is on a higher, and thus more important, plane than the material world. The material world of the body, passions, and emotions is regarded as something base, dispensable, and the source of evil temptations. The real self that must be saved is separate from the body and all that it experiences. In such a view, the body, and all material things, must be disciplined, kept under control, and even punished, for the sake of attaining a higher state of life and achieving the spiritual end of "saving the soul."

Another approach to spirituality that stands out in striking contrast to the ascetical austerities that separate matter and spirit is the incarnational spirituality of Zorba the Greek, that memorable character of Nikos Kazantzakis's life-affirming novel by the same title.[2] Whether working in a mine, confronting monks, or making love, Zorba's life is rich with all the joys and sorrows that life brings. He is madly in love with life, exuberant, and ready to dance at the sound of a downbeat. He knows what to do with a good bottle of wine, and how to pray and play as the occasion warrants. Zorba's spirituality is not about some other kind of life standing over against this one, but it is about all that belongs to being human. It represents a thirst for wholeness without taking on self-imposed punishments. While Zorba's spirituality is attractive for the way it engages the whole person in all of life's experiences, it can be self-absorbed, deceptive of one's need for conversion, and misleading about how ascetical disciplines of self-denial can be a positive means for growing in love and wholeness and not obstacles to it.

Sally Mae represents yet another approach to spirituality that fits roughly into the contemplative tradition. I first met her in the parish in 1970. She is a wife and a stay-at-home mom of two daughters. Everyone in the parish knew her as the "contemplative" one. Her version of the contemplative approach to spirituality consisted largely of devotional practices. Each morning, she would silently slide into the back pew for Mass, and then always stay afterward to complete her holy hour. During Lent she added the Stations of the Cross to her morning ritual. Whenever the parish held any special devotional services, penance services, parish missions, or weekend retreats, Sally Mae was there with her rosary, her holy hour book, a packet of holy cards of saints with prayers on the back, and a well-worn devotional book of prayers and readings.

The contemplative approach to spirituality has the great advantage of holding before us the goal of spiritual striving— union with God. Its danger is escaping from the world and human concerns. Thomas Merton comes to mind as one who lived as a contemplative but with an intense sensitivity for the deepest yearnings of life. He taught us that contemplative spirituality that is deaf to the cries of humanity is like an incomplete sentence. It risks reducing spirituality to a myopic "me and God" exercise of saving one's soul without including the lives of those who suffer.

If escapism is the danger of a contemplative approach to spirituality, then activism is the danger of the spirituality that makes works of charity and justice its core. While the contemplative risks losing touch with the world, the social activist risks losing touch with God. Take Billy Joe, for example. He was raised Catholic and came of age in the '60s when the church opened its windows on the world and the civil rights and antiwar movements were seizing the American conscience. He became deeply involved in movements to achieve racial integration, to improve wages and working conditions for farm workers, and to bring about peace in Vietnam. His passion for justice outdistanced his spiritual practices. In time, he gave up being a practicing Catholic but never lost his fascination with the writings of Dorothy Day and Thomas Merton. He remains committed to social reform and is actively involved in trying to help the homeless. But what Billy Joe is missing is what Dorothy Day and Thomas Merton witnessed—namely, the dynamic of turning outward in solidarity with all that yearns for fulfillment cannot be detached from the dynamic of prayer moving inward to remain rooted in God.

Each of these models—the ascetical, the incarnational, the contemplative, and the social activist—complements the other. Each can be an effective springboard to virtue, as the lives of the saints through the ages have shown. Another approach to spirituality tries to integrate the best features of these models in such a way that it cannot be characterized as any one of these approaches. This is what Mary Jane witnesses. She is a wife and the soccer mom of three boys. She regularly attends the 11:00 A.M. Sunday Mass. I met her when she was chairing the social action committee of the parish. Professionally, Mary Jane is the director of human resources for an electronics firm located in the parish. Other parishioners who work in the same firm say that they do not want a day to go by without having a chance to see Mary Jane. She is a calm oasis in the midst of frenetic activity. A few moments with her energy, attitude, humor, and attentiveness brighten one's day. Some would like to say that she is a very "holy" person, but they don't want that notion to be mistaken for sanctimony. Mary Jane is certainly not like that. When I asked what makes them think that she is holy, they answered that they feel "holy" in her presence. They touch a deeper center in themselves because she relates to them from a center of peace in herself. When I asked Mary Jane how she was able to manage so many responsibilities with such grace and yet to be present to people in such an effective way, she said that it is her "quiet time" each day that gets her focused and helps her to be present to whatever comes her way. She starts her day knowing to whom she belongs and to what she is committed. Her identity is secure.

For Mary Jane, spirituality connects to the "something more" or to the "depth dimension" of human experience. This is what some refer to as the "inner meaning" of life, or the "deeper reasons" that motivate a person. We can touch into the depth dimension of life, for example, in those times when we are moved by a sunset or music, or when we are shocked by the devastations of war or other acts of violence, or when we are touched by random acts of uncommon kindness by people who expect no reward, or when we are struck by an unconditional offer of forgiveness, or when we are inspired by the courageous endurance of serious illness or the calm acceptance of death, or when we are moved by a parent nurturing a child. Experiences such as these connect us to a level of reality that is greater than the present moment and to a deeper mystery than meets the eye. A spiritual practice such as Mary Jane's contemplative prayer helps us to attend to this depth dimension of our life and to recognize our basic beliefs, root values, and fundamental outlook on life. Those who live out of their center manifest their spirituality in a style of life characterized by an attentive presence to what is going on, by a nondefensive posture in the face of criticism, by peace of mind when facing situations of great ambiguity, and by a sense of hope that goodness will prevail even in the face of evil, tragedy, or death.

These are only a few approaches to spirituality. What else would you add? I have caricatured these models a bit to sharpen the point. Remember, the aim here is to try to come to some understanding of what we are talking about when we talk about spirituality. There is no one way to express one's spirituality, and there is no single, universally agreed upon meaning of spirituality or, more specifically, "Christian spirituality." In the Appendix of the opening chapter, "Christian Spirituality," in their book by the same name, Lawrence Cunningham and Keith Egan list twenty-three different definitions of spirituality and/or Christian spirituality.[3] It seems that everyone who writes about spirituality has his or her own definition for this dimension of life. At present, there is not, and perhaps there cannot be, an exhaustive and all-embracing definition of spirituality. But what we assume to be included in spirituality will influence how we see its relationship to morality. So we need some working definition.

To put it simply, spirituality expresses a way of life animated by the longings of a restless human spirit. Or, to be more formal about it, *spirituality designates a way of living that strives to integrate our diverse experiences into a meaningful whole by connecting all of life to what we believe gives ultimate meaning and value to our lives.*[4]

What gives ultimate value answers our deepest desire, our most urgent longing—to find meaning. This desire for meaning is the most easily recognized form of spiritual hunger. Without meaning, our life wanders aimlessly and our self-worth erodes. Meaning in life comes from the sum of the loves in our life. There's no other source. Only when we live with love do we truly live. Love makes our hearts rail against meaninglessness. Spirituality is ultimately about how we connect with what counts most for us in living.

No one has the luxury of choosing whether they want to have a spirituality or not. Everyone has one. It is not just for those who seem to have a particular bent for it. We all live with some sense of meaning, though we differ on just what it is and where to find it. Some find it in religion, others in the stars, and still others in a commitment to peace and justice, to protecting the environment, or to saving the whales. Wherever it is that we find meaning, spirituality follows as the way we make sense out of what is happening to us and around us so that we do not become undone. The opposite of having a spirituality is to lose one's soul, to live without love, to be disconnected and unglued, to drop out and to wander aimlessly.

Whether we want it to or not, our spirituality shows itself in and through everything that we do and all the relationships that make up our lives. We recognize our spirituality from the outside in. Indices of our spirituality, for example, are such behaviors as whether we sleep at night or toss and turn, whether we have to rely on tranquilizers to get us through the day or not, whether we live in harmony with our bodies or out of touch with them, whether we are loving or bitter, whether we are giving ourselves over to God and the poor or to drug-induced highs and the fast track. Spirituality is the center of our lives, and it is capable of "bubbling up" everywhere. It lies behind our outlook on life and gets expressed in our ways of coping with life. It is also a powerful force influencing our evaluation of the possible courses of action we can take so as to live with meaning and integrity. This partly explains how some disagreements in ethics are, at root, often matters of spirituality. The disagreements over how to respond to T.K. in the case from the Introduction are less about differences in methods of decision making and more about differences about what counts most in life. Since spirituality also shows itself in the style of life through which we express our basic attitudes, convictions, and emotions, no aspect of our lives escapes the influence of our spirituality. It is like the seasoning that flavors the sauce. It expresses who we are and what we genuinely believe, for spirituality is where we ultimately integrate the diverse experiences of our life into a meaningful whole.

Understood in this way, spirituality characterizes both those who believe in God and those who do not. There is nothing particularly religious about it. A secular humanist could endorse it. So what makes spirituality religious, or, more specifically, Christian? Christian spirituality is that specific form of religious spirituality that presupposes belief in a personal, loving God, revealed in Jesus through the Holy Spirit in the community of the church. Christian spirituality is life in God's Spirit. It is possible because God has taken the initiative in loving us and continues to be at work in us. Christian spirituality began with God giving us the Holy Spirit through the resurrection of Jesus with the intent of transforming every dimension of our life through the same Holy Spirit—our work, our leisure, our civic duties and home life, our health and well-being. At the basis of Christian spirituality, then, is a personal experience of God as our ultimate value, reaching out to us in love through the Holy Spirit and inviting us and leading us to the fullness of life in communion with divine love. In brief, then, Christian spirituality is about our living through faith in relationship with God's Spirit.

While spirituality includes our response to God, it begins with God loving us first, preeminently in Jesus but also in and through all the people and events of our lives. In every experience we are already involved with God and drawn to God. With God as our starting point, we see all things in God and respond to God in and through all things. As a response, spirituality entails a morality, a way of life, a life lived with a certain spirit—

in the case of the Christian spiritual life, a life lived in the spirit of Jesus.

The discipline that studies the experience of God and the various traditions, ways of life, and practices that have emerged to express our response to God is also called "spirituality." Spiritualities (plural) are the distinctively different set of beliefs, stories, and practices people have developed to stay in touch with the spiritual dimension of their lives.

Sandra Schneiders has suggested that we could simplify the discussion of what Christian spirituality is about by agreeing that the referent of the term *spirituality* is "Christian religious experience."[5] As "Christian," it is affected by all of our theological convictions that shape our framework of meaning, such as our convictions about God, Jesus, and the human person, as well as how these get expressed in worship and in our lifestyle. Our spirituality changes as we nourish our theological convictions through spiritual and moral practices, such as prayer, worship, and social service, and try to integrate new perceptions and convictions into the whole context of our life. Moreover, as Christian, spirituality is a way of discipleship involving a personal relationship with Jesus under the power of the Holy Spirit working in and through the community of believers to bring about a world marked by justice and peace. In this sense, Christian spirituality is not fully understood as a person's subjective dispositions, nor is it sustained entirely on one's own. Holiness is a cooperative adventure. Thus, we can expect Christian spirituality to come with the notice we often find on boxes of Christmas toys—Some Assembly Required. Christian spirituality is ultimately communitarian. Without some involvement in a community of faith, we can too easily make spirituality the working out of a private agenda rather than a way of discipleship. Christian spirituality requires stable, enduring relationships with a community of faith that shares common practices and stable convictions about who we are and who God is in Jesus and through the Spirit. The community's discernment can keep us honest about whether we are becoming who we profess to be as disciples of Jesus.

As "religious," Christian spirituality has both intellectual and affective dimensions. These are nurtured and expressed in the ways that we address God in prayer and ritual. The religious dimension takes us beyond an intellectual acknowledgment that God is self-giving love to an affective appreciation that God loves me. Moreover, the religious aspect of Christian spirituality must hold in balance a sense of transcendence and immanence. An overemphasis on the transcendent, as we saw with Simeon Stylites and Sally Mae, reduces spirituality to one's relationship with God and can lead to ignoring one's daily tasks and social relationships for the sake of a deeper interior life. An overemphasis on immanence, as we saw with Zorba and Billy Joe, can reduce spirituality to some form of self-absorbing therapy or social action. Christian spirituality as religious must remain rooted in the world while accepting that there is more than meets the eye, as it does for Francis of Assisi, Dorothy Day, Thomas Merton, and Mary Jane.

As "experience," Christian spirituality cannot be limited to moments of prayer or the interior movements aroused in prayer.

It must encompass whatever enters into the actual living of our lives—daily events and tasks, family and social relationships, hopes and fears, work and play, health and illness, birth and death. Christian spirituality refers primarily not to having extraordinary experiences but to how we handle ordinary, day-to-day experiences. When we take the experiential dimension seriously, there can be no disjunction between the spiritual and the human. They work together in such a way that the spiritual is expressed in and through the human. In this way, our spirituality is shaped by our response to what comes our way in the course of living day by day. The widespread interest in spiritual direction can be explained, in part, by a growing appreciation that we can understand what is happening in our relationship with God to the extent that we understand what is happening in our experiences. The reason we can speak of different kinds of Christian spirituality (lay, marital, clerical, monastic, feminist, African American, and others) is that different experiences are the context for meeting God and responding to God.

In summary, then, when we talk about spirituality, we mean how we will relate to what we believe gives ultimate meaning and value to our everyday lives. Spirituality polishes the lens whereby we see more clearly in order to walk more rightly according to the vision of life that our ultimate value gives us. Christian spirituality integrates life around the personal experience that God, our ultimate value, values us. Jesus is our model and the inspiration of what life can look like when we entrust our lives to God and take to heart that God loves us.

Morality

If the spiritual dimension of being human pertains to seeing all things in relation to what we believe gives ultimate value, the moral dimension, by contrast, pertains to our effort to flourish as persons and communities in response to our ultimate value. The terms of reference for morality are the *person* expressing one's self in *action*. Morality engages our capacity both to make someone of ourselves and to determine the kind of actions we ought to perform. In a nutshell, morality is about what we should do because of who we are. Or, to be more formal about it, *morality is about acquiring those virtues and doing those actions that enhance the full flourishing of human life in community and in harmony with the environment.* Morality asks, "Who should I be?" and "What should I do?" so that we can live together in peace and harmony with one another and with our environment.

Understood in this way, morality has no particularly religious aspect, and "ethics" is the common way of referring to the disciplined way of thinking about who is a good person and what are right and wrong actions. When God is included as a necessary and fixed point of reference, then morality takes on a religious dimension, and moral theology, or theological ethics, is the way to name its disciplined study.

Of morality's two terms of reference—person and action— more often than not, people associate morality with actions. The moral quandary posed in the Introduction fits well into many people's notion of what morality is all about—solving problems in such a way that we "do the right thing." If we restrict the meaning of morality to problems and right actions, we focus merely on how we should treat others and on the rules or principles that should guide and justify our conduct. Do I have a moral obligation to treat a terminal patient? What is my duty to my aging parents? Am I morally bound to pay all my taxes? Do I have a moral obligation to fulfill my promise? The focus of morality, then, becomes problems to solve and the strategies we use (principles or consequences) to determine the actions that will solve the problems. Such an understanding reflects a legal model for morality.

One of the great limitations of the legal model is that it turns the moral life into a series of "cases" requiring decisions. That is to say, we do not think of ourselves as living the moral life except when we are solving problems by following rational procedures. Living morally becomes a matter of determining the right thing to do by appealing to some abstract, universal principle, as though we were permitted to make some disinterested judgment from a neutral standpoint. In such a view, all those components of character, such as our convictions, intentions, perspective, emotions, commitments, cultural and religious background, past history, or future plans, seem to have nothing to do with the way we ought to act now.

In many ways, it is quite understandable that so many people think about morality as occasionalistic, analogous to law, and oriented toward solving a problem. Certainly, we need commonly accepted rules if we are going to ensure harmonious relations among diverse people. Moreover, in the Catholic tradition, as chapter 2 will show, centuries of maintaining a functional relationship between moral theology and the sacrament of penance has instilled the legal model of the moral life in the Catholic consciousness. Haunting questions, like "What do I have to do?" "Is it allowed?" and "How far can I go?" echoed in our consciences. Unfortunately, the necessary role of law in correcting our inconstancy and instructing our ignorance has given way to a legal mentality that sees everything in legal terms—God is the supreme lawgiver, living morally is governed by laws, obedience to authority is our principal virtue, loyalty is measured by obedience, and we live in order to receive a reward (heaven) or to avoid punishment (hell).

The legal mentality gives the impression that morality is episodic and primarily about actions governed by rules that someone else has imposed on us for the sake of controlling our behavior. But moral imperatives (the "must" and "ought") do not come in the first instance from some rule externally imposed. The *ought* in "I ought to" comes from the nature of being human in relationship. The demand to be good and to do what is right arises from being in the presence of another. We tell the truth because of our commitment to the other person; we care about them and do not want to deceive them. In this sense, we experience the other as an invitation to come out of ourselves and relate in ways that will enable everyone to flourish in their humanity. Rules or laws (Be truthful, Do not lie) emerge later as expressions of what experience has shown are reliable ways to protect the dignity of persons, to give stability to social relationships, and to live in harmony with the environment. So morality is not to be thought of as being just about actions (doing the right thing) but primarily about persons (being good). The more adequate understanding of the moral life is not mere obedience to law but fidelity to life-giving personal relationships.

When we begin with relationships rather than the law, we can better appreciate how morality is fundamentally social. Morality expresses our responsibility for the relationships that constitute our lives so that there is no split between the person and society. Since the very identity of the individual is conceived in terms of his or her relationships, "private morality" is a contradiction in terms. To be a moral person means that we are searching for ways to live together that will enable everyone to flourish. After all, our lives are constituted by relationships and by our response to those relationships. That we must relate to others is inevitable. How we respond to them is a matter of character and choice.

A relational-responsibility oriented morality[6] is born in the heart. It begins with a sensitive awareness of the worth of another. Not to sense the moral call that the preciousness of another makes in our presence is to have an underdeveloped heart. To lack such empathy is to be morally paralyzed. No wonder those who have been emotionally traumatized lack any feeling of responsibility toward others. They get closed in upon themselves. Not until we are able to experience the other as distinct from ourselves and worthy of our careful attention will we be able to act upon values that protect and promote the well-being not only of that one other but of all living things. Moral living, then, expresses our sensitivity to what this perception of preciousness requires of us so that we can contribute to the full flourishing of persons and community in harmony with the environment.

Thus far there is nothing specifically religious or Christian about this description of the moral dimension of being human. It can be said of anyone. No reasonable atheist could object to it. What makes it religious and Christian is our belief that the One to whom we are ultimately responding in and through all of the relationships of our life is God, revealed in Jesus as the love we ultimately desire. So whether we experience God, how we experience God, and what beliefs we hold about God will have a pervasive, though not exclusive, effect on the sort of person we are and on what we do. For Christian believers, morality expresses the experience that we have of knowing and being loved by God. In this sense, the moral life is like worship. It is a response to the experience of God, and so it is spiritual in its roots.

For the Christian, then, morality cannot but be closely related to spirituality, to experiences of God, and to beliefs about God. The Christian cannot do justice to his or her moral experience and moral worldview without seeing all things as being related to God in some way as the source and goal of it all. Christian morality has a desired and anticipated end—union with God. In fact, God is the horizon against which the believer sees and values all things. As a result, the morality of those whose imagination is influenced by the experience of God and the beliefs of the Judeo-Christian tradition about God has a distinctively spiritual-theological element to it. The very purpose of the moral life is to live in the Spirit of God in imitation of Christ.

Moreover, morality for the religious believer is not authorized merely by social convention, or merely by the desire for self-fulfillment, or merely by the requirements of general rules of conduct that reason demands. Though all of these are legitimate ways to authorize morality, they are not sufficient from a theological point of view. From a theological point of view, God authorizes and requires morality. As a result, moral responsibilities are not merely to oneself or to other persons, nor are they only to the demands of rationality. They are, rather, responsibilities to God. The moral call to be good and to do what is right that arises from our encounter with the other is always a call from God (cf. Matt 25). So everyday relationships and mundane acts are not separate from our spirituality and moral life but are very much a part of them. They are, theologically speaking, acts of worship. That is, they participate in responding to God's purpose for life as revealed in Jesus and kept alive in the Spirit.

"God loves you!" is at the core of Christian revelation. Believing that God loves us is perhaps our most difficult act of faith. Yet, it is our first step in moral living. It is not what we do but rather what God first does on our behalf (grace) that is the bedrock upon which we can build a moral life. God's love for us is an invitation to love God in return by imitating God's love revealed in Jesus. Our responding to God is possible in the first place because God has taken the initiative to love us through acting in creation, pre-eminently in Jesus, but most immediately through all the people and events of our lives.

One of the ways that we can interpret the scene of Jesus' baptism as recorded in the Synoptic Gospels is that through it Jesus experienced an incredible affirmation of being loved by God: "You are my Son, the Beloved; with you I am well pleased" (Luke 3:22; Mark 1:11; Matt 3:17). Because Jesus was able to take this assertion to heart, he was able to make his life what he did. He never lost touch with his truth; he knew whose he was, so he lived under the blessing of his Father. Unfortunately, not all of us can claim the same for ourselves. But if we allowed ourselves to be affected by God's love for us, then we too could live confidently under God's blessing and love God in return. As with growth in any true love, as we come to know what is important to the beloved, we seek to love what the beloved loves. This is so not only in human love but in our love for God as well.[7]

So, the first major feature of the Christian moral life is that it is grounded religiously (in an experience of God) and is expressed as worship (a response to God). The ultimate purpose of the Christian moral life is to love God and be forever in union with God. The moral mandate to love God is enshrined in the first of the Ten Commandments and it is summarized in the first part of the Great Commandment: "You shall love the Lord your God with all your heart, with all your soul, and with all your mind" (Matt 22:37). We show that we love God when we pray as well as when we cooperate with God by caring for what God cares about. In taking time for prayer, we make a conscious, intentional effort to direct our awareness to God. When we pray, we attend to loving God more directly than when we are loving our neighbor. Edward Vacek has insightfully distinguished loving God and loving neighbor in such a way that each is related to the other but one is not identified with the other: "We should love God directly, we should love our neighbor as an overflow of our love for God, and we should love God in and through loving our neighbor."[8] Thus, the other part of the Great Commandment is inseparably linked to loving God but is not identical with it: "You shall love your neighbor as yourself" (Matt 22:39).

Putting the two parts of the Great Commandment together, then, makes the moral life spiritual at its source and the spiritual life moral in its manifestations. That is, the love of neighbor and self are ultimately grounded in our love for God. We have expressed this liturgically in the ancient prayer to the Spirit: "Come Holy Spirit, fill the hearts of your faithful. And kindle in them the fire of your love." This process of loving God and caring about what God cares about presumes an active prayer life, nurtured by scripture, supported by the community's common prayer, and tested within a community of discernment. Those whose moral life is born out of the experience of God's love and that is nurtured by spiritual practices can and ought to be able to discern what God is enabling and requiring them to be and to do.

How do we know what God's love for us is calling us to be and to do right now? Where do we look to find God? We look right into the heart of those places where we are living our lives, especially the relationships that make up our lives. James Keenan has argued that we are relational in three ways: generally, specifically, and uniquely. Each demands a cardinal virtue in response. As a relational being in general, we need justice; our specific relationships call us to fidelity; the unique relationship we have with ourselves calls us to self-care. Living in response to God requires the prudential discernment of what constitutes the just, faithful, and self-caring way of life we ought to follow.[9] So morality is best understood not as a set of laws imposed from without, but as a dynamic expression of virtue responding to the experience of being loved by God. Character and virtue are where morality and spirituality converge.

In the process of becoming virtuous, morality is more concerned with what is happening to the person performing actions than with the actions the person performs. William Spohn has it exactly right when he reflects on the relation of character and decisions:

> Most of the "work" of the moral life happens before we get to the moments of decision. The quality of our lives between decisions will determine what we see, how we are affected, how truthfully we examine our options, and consequently what we decide. The quality of our lives will determine our ability to discern.[10]

Spohn has captured here an insight that goes back to Aristotle: we are what we do habitually.[11] The moral quality of our lives does not lie in the occasional, dramatic decisions that we sometimes have to make, but in the character that we have formed by living from day to day doing things over and over again. This daily living creates a certain degree of moral momentum in the habits that express our character. For example, we wouldn't expect a liar suddenly to tell the truth, a slanderer to break forth into paeans of praise, or a domineering and controlling boss to have a fit of collaboration. How we behave in a crucial moment is born out of the habits we form from the way we behave in the day-to-day course of our lives. So, if we want to make a virtuous decision in hard times, then we need to develop the habit of virtue in daily affairs. The moral life goes on continually. We don't switch it on and off with the occasional moral choice.

Character gives us moral continuity. It is our tendency to feel, think, and act with a certain degree of consistency and so gives stability and an abiding quality to our lives. Our character, or moral identity, involves our sense of direction established over time and continues to be demonstrated through the pattern of actions we perform, the vision we have of life, the convictions or beliefs we live by, the intentions we seek to fulfill, the dispositions that ready us to act as well as the affections and motivations that move us to do what we believe to be right. Character explains not merely why we act in a certain way now but why we can be counted on to act that way in the future. With considerable momentum that does not go into reverse easily, character has a kind of stability. Since we generally stay "in character," people can detect patterns to our actions. Likewise, atypical behavior is suspect because it is so "uncharacteristic."

This focus on character and virtue (those dispositions of heart and mind to act in a certain way) takes seriously that who we are affects what we do, and what we do affects who we become. This is the very lesson Forrest Gump's mother taught him early on in life when she said, "Stupid is as stupid does." If we do something well, we become better; if we do it poorly, we become worse. If we drive like a maniac, chances are we will become one. If we treat our friends with respect, chances are we will become respectful and treat even strangers respectfully in turn. But if we treat friends in a condescending manner, then we will likely become arrogant and patronizing and so treat others in a condescending manner as well. The way we act now will affect how we act later. If we want to be a better person, then, we need to recognize and to take the opportunities we have to do better. That is to say, if we want to be more loving, peaceful, gentle, sincere, and friendly, then we have to act in those ways when we have the chance. Our choices and actions will either deepen our already existing habits and so strengthen our character, or will create new habits and so modify our character. Our character, while stable, is not fixed in stone. We are all works in progress. No one is finished. Conversion is always possible, whereby one's perception of the world, one's convictions or intentions will be changed, and one's character refashioned.

In contrast to the act-centered approach to morality that asks, "What is the right thing to do?" a morality focused on character and virtue asks, "From what inner place are you doing it?" In answering this question, morality meets spirituality. While actions are important in either approach to morality, the character of a person is crucial to the morality of the action focused on virtue, for character is the source of perspective in judging what to do and of the steadiness of intention for doing it.

Being formed in virtue makes us morally fit to meet our daily responsibilities. With virtue, we acquire sensitivity to values that we have internalized and so acquire a readiness to act in a certain way because of who we are. Virtue gives us a cognitive advantage to know what is right and an emotional predisposition to do it. Virtues influence how we assess what is going on. Cognitively, we speak of virtuous people as having a "nose" or a "special sense" for what is right. The morally good person knows the right thing to do, not so much through refined moral analysis or dependence on external rules, but by feeling a resonance or harmony between one's own being and the act to be done. Emotionally, virtuous people will want to do what is right and avoid what is wrong because virtues make them affectively committed to certain values. The virtuous person, for example, who has developed a habit of being sensitive to others has an interior compass pointing to what fits a person in need and then acts on it somewhat spontaneously. Rules may point to such an action as right, but rules are not the first recourse for the virtuous. Well-established habits are. Character, in a sense, chooses for them.

In sum, morality asks, "What should we do because of who we are?" For Christians, our character and choices ought to be a dynamic expression of the experience of being loved by God and sustained by God through our commitment to Christ, the full revelation of God. Moral living is moving conscientiously toward the goal of union with God by living in the Spirit of God revealed in Jesus. The challenge for us is to give concrete expression to what being faithful to God in the imitation of Christ would look like in our contemporary circumstances. As the incarnational principle tells us, only through the human will we come to know what God is enabling and requiring us to be and to do. Morality, then, must take seriously critical reflection on the experience of human relationships as the source for discerning what is required of us.

Spirituality and Morality

Given what has just been described as the spiritual and moral dimensions of human life, we can see a little more clearly where the points of convergence might be. A long time ago, spirituality and morality went their separate ways. Chapter 2 will give an account of this divorce in greater detail. It will show that one of the reasons for the separation was that morality became too preoccupied with actions and left concern for the person to spirituality. But that is all changing now. It is time that we put back together what belongs together. Spirituality's drive toward integrating the whole of one's life around what gives ultimate value and morality's emphasis on the centrality of personal character and virtue offer a point of convergence for spirituality and morality.

By way of conclusion to this chapter, I want to give a brief glimpse of this convergence by retrieving some of the key notions that express what we mean by spirituality and morality. The basic unity of Christian spirituality and morality is related to their common starting point and goal—the experience of God and union with God. Whether we experience God and how we experience God will have a great influence on the content and quality of our spirituality and moral life. Christian spirituality is centered on the experience of God's loving us in Christ and through the Spirit in the church. Spiritual practices, such as vocal prayers, meditating on scripture, and rituals of worship like the Eucharist, can nurture a way of life centered on God's love for us and our love for God.

Christian morality is rooted in the experience of God's love (spirituality) and expresses our response to the love of God for us in moral practices of virtue, such as honoring the self through appropriate self-care, helping our neighbor in need, working for justice, or protecting the environment. The sort of person we ought to be and how we ought to behave in the world as a result of our experience of God remain the central concern of morality. The fully human response to the love of God is revealed in Jesus. In the moral life, we follow Jesus as disciples alive in his spirit. Our encounter with Jesus through the spiritual practice of meditating on his words and deeds as recorded in the Gospels, for example, can have a formative influence on our moral life. The key question, then, for relating spirituality and morality, is this: Who should we be and how should we live if we believe that God loves us and that we love God?

Spirituality can never be separated from morality as some external aid that helps us be good. Spirituality, with its array of practices, nourishes the moral life at its very roots by deepening our awareness of being loved and by energizing our commitment to living in a way that makes this love a real, transforming presence in the world. Spirituality is the wellspring of the moral life. That is to say that morality arises from, rather than generates, spirituality. The moral journey begins in that spiritual space where we accept God's love for us and awaken to responsibility for promoting the well-being of persons and the community in harmony with the environment. In this way, morality reveals one's spirituality. In other words, how we live reveals who we are, what we genuinely value, and how we are integrating life experiences around what gives ultimate value. To reduce spirituality to the interior life apart from its public expression is to fall back on some kind of dualism. But we do not respond to God by some disembodied, internal word of acceptance or refusal. We respond with all dimensions of our self. Spirituality's drive toward integration and morality's response to God includes all aspects of life and pervades the whole of a person's identity—one's convictions, feelings, perspective, motivations, attitudes, and behavior. There is no area untouched by spirituality.

While we might want to distinguish the respective interests of spirituality and morality by focusing spirituality on our relationship to God and morality on who to be and how to behave in the world, we ought not to separate them so much that we lose their mutual influence on one another. In fact, spirituality so pervades morality that differences between moral judgments and lifestyles can often be explained by different spiritualities. We may hold to the same principles, use the same method of argument, do the same moral practices, but we can ultimately differ because we have different outlooks on life, different assumptions about what befits human well-being, different priorities of value, different depths of passion and zeal for common values, and a different vision of what life is ultimately all about. These are basically differences in spirituality that influence our morality. Morality can influence spirituality, too. Our involvement in working for justice, for example, can awaken us to examine our inner motivations and source of our commitment to justice in the first place, and it can send us back to engage spiritual practices that focus us on the deeper dimensions that unite us to one another and that lead us to our ultimate dependence on a source of life and love greater than us.

What Are We Talking About?

This brief preview of the relation of spirituality and morality suggests that they function in a critical-dialogical relationship. This means that they shape and reshape one another. While spirituality gives rise to morality, morality in turn reacts upon spirituality to correct or to confirm its direction. A sign of an authentic spirituality is the kind of life it engenders. As the biblical criterion would have it, "You will know them by their fruits" (Matt 7:20). Morality is the public face of one's spirituality, for morality is the place where we express our experience of God and our response to God. Without spirituality, morality gets cut off from its roots in the experience of God and so loses its character as a personal response to being loved by God, or being graced. Then it easily gets reduced to abiding by laws and to solving moral problems. Likewise, without morality, spirituality can spin off into ethereal ideas that never become real. Then the criticisms of spirituality as being about some other life in some other world would be true. But spirituality permeates all aspects of morality. It is the atmosphere within which we form and express our virtue.

Recent developments in moral theology give us the context and concepts for understanding this relationship more clearly. The next chapter will show that we have for too long kept spirituality separate from morality. It is time to put back together what belongs together.

2.

Where Have We Been?

❁

For too long, spirituality and morality have gone their separate ways. But the divorce is over now and a remarriage is underway. The conviction of this book is that there really is no moral life separate from a spiritual life. Because of the interconnectedness that seems obvious to so many today, one might expect that spiritual theology and moral theology were always closely aligned and mutually influencing one another. But that has not been the case, at least in any sustained and conscious way. This chapter will try to provide a brief sketch of the historical highlights of the marriage, divorce, and remarriage of spirituality and morality as an aid to putting back together what belongs together.

Marriage

The Bible knows no separation of the spiritual life and the moral life. The great covenant between God and Israel encompassed the whole of life. It involves a commitment to respond to God's invitation of love in and through all that makes up one's life. In the covenant, practicing the presence of God becomes central to moral responsibility and spiritual growth. When the prophets call the people back to the covenant, they call them back both to right living and to right worship.

In Jesus, the New Covenant, we find the same all encompassing call. The way of discipleship is to imitate Jesus in his loyal obedience to God and in self-giving service of others. For the true disciple there is no separation between moral and spiritual striving. This is captured in the Pauline notion of the Christian life as being "in Christ" (1 Cor 1:30) and in the Johannine emphasis on the unity of the love of God and of neighbor (1 John 4:20). No one can claim to be "in Christ" or to have an authentic spiritual life—a loving relationship with God—apart from loving actions and relationships in one's daily life. The Christian moral life is well integrated with the spiritual life.

The theology of the patristic era was conceived as a unity to which the later subdivisions into dogmatic and moral theology were totally foreign. The unifying feature was the Bible. Theology was, by and large, something along the order of what we would call today biblical spirituality, that is, reflection on scripture with the aim of coming to a fuller understanding of Christian faith and a deepening of the Christian life in all its aspects. Reflection, prayer, and living were all of a piece. Because patristic theology encompassed exegesis, doctrinal speculation, contemplation, and morality, we find in it an integration of the moral and spiritual life.

From the sixth to twelfth centuries, the medieval monastic theology carried forward this patristic synthesis with its style of doing theology from a meditative reading, reflecting, and commenting on scripture and the Fathers of the Church known as *lectio divina*. What would later be called "spiritual theology" continued to appear in the context of homilies or scriptural commentaries. Medieval readers of scripture based themselves on a theory of interpretation going back to Origen's (ca. 185–254) threefold sense of scripture (literal, typological, and spiritual). John Cassian (ca. 360–435) developed Origen's method in his four senses of the text. There was the literal sense that considered the biblical events as historical realities, and three "spiritual" senses—the allegorical sense revealed the theological meaning of the text; the tropological sense applied the text to moral living; and the anagogical sense focused on the ultimate or finally realized meaning of the text.[1] The unifying feature of this way of doing theology was obviously the Bible, and the assumption that contemporary lives were in continuity with the biblical stories. Spirituality and morality were not far apart as long as the Bible was the common context and object of study, prayer, and life. In the hands of great theological interpreters of scripture like Origen, Augustine, or Bernard of Clairvaux, the spiritual interpretation of scripture was a way of delving into the divine mysteries and finding guidance for a way of life faithful to the gospel.

Divorce

But the patristic and medieval theological writings were not the major influence on the subsequent development of moral theology and its gradual drifting away from spirituality. The evolution of the sacrament of penance was. The divorce of morality from spirituality is rooted in a preoccupation with sins in pastoral texts and in the pastoral ministry. The nature and focus of three kinds of literature contributed to the isolation of morality from spirituality and have shaped the discipline we know today as moral theology: the Irish monastic penitentials, the *summae confessorum*, and the moral manuals.

The Penitentials

According to John Mahoney in his magisterial work on the history of moral theology, *The Making of Moral Theology*, "There is no doubt that the single most influential factor in the development of the practice and of the discipline of moral theology is to be found in the growth and spread of 'confession' in the Church."[2] As a result, the body of literature that emerged to guide the practice of penance from the sixth century to the twentieth has had the greatest influence on shaping the tone and interest of moral theology and on separating morality from spirituality.

At first, however, the separation was not so sharp. The *libri paenitentiales*, or penitential books, began to appear in the sixth century as the handiwork of monks in the Celtic and Anglo-Saxon churches. These books reflected a close connection between the moral and spiritual life in the way they encouraged moral conversion and spiritual growth. This came about through a unique blending of the monastic practice of spiritual direction, wherein one revealed one's conscience and faults to a "soul friend," and the rise of individual private confession.

Monastic practice favored a monk's having an *anmchara* (a soul friend), or as we would say today a "spiritual director," with whom to share one's commitments and failings in living the

Christian life. "Anyone without a soul friend is like a body without a head" is believed to have been a popular adage in the Celtic church.[3] Some soul friends were nonordained men, some were women. But a common expectation of the monastic church was that everyone ought to have this special person in one's life to whom one could manifest one's conscience and seek spiritual guidance. The soul friend was essentially a guide in one's spiritual quest, and the role was not regarded in specifically sacramental terms, as we might think of it. In this unique context, the Irish Christian could manifest his or her conscience to the soul friend, who would in turn prescribe ascetical practices for the purpose of spiritual growth.

Out of this practice among the monks grew the private penitent-confessor relationship, which became an important aspect of the monk's pastoral ministry. As lay people began to turn to the monks for advice and spiritual counsel, the monks naturally used with them the very forms to which they themselves had grown accustomed in the monastery. The ingenious wedding of the practice of spiritual direction with private confession inaugurated a form of confessional practice that has occasioned the development of our modern practice of penance.

The penitentials were developed by the monks to provide confessors with a guide to the kind of penances or spiritual disciplines that would suit penitents in all sorts of moral and spiritual predicaments and according to their social and ecclesial status. For example, in the *Penitential of Finnian* (ca. 525–550), the earliest document thought to be a complete penitential book, we find this:

If anyone has started a quarrel and plotted in his heart to strike or kill his neighbor, if the offender is a cleric, he shall do penance for half a year with an allowance of bread and water and for a whole year abstain from wine and meats, and thus he will be reconciled to the altar.

But if he is a layman, he shall do penance for a week, since he is a man of this world and his guilt is lighter in this world and his reward less in the world to come.[4]

The role of the penance in this early practice was to be "health-giving medicine of souls," as the beginning of the *Penitential of Cummean* (ca. 650) has it.[5] Healing or the "cure of souls" was the primary metaphor that directed this practice of penance in its early stages. Later attitudes toward penance as a penalty for a crime represented a deterioration of this monastic spirit. The healing metaphor for penances is exemplified by the principle of contraries whereby a vice is cured by applying a contrary virtue. Again in the *Penitential of Finnian* we find the principle used like this:

But by contraries, as we said, let us make haste to cure contraries and to cleanse away the faults from our hearts and introduce virtues in their places. Patience must arise for wrathfulness; kindliness, or the love of God and of one's neighbor, for envy; for detraction, restraint of heart and tongue; for dejection, spiritual joy; for greed, liberality....[6]

The principle of contraries regards sins as diseases of the soul, and so penances are prescribed to counter the disease and to promote healing. In this way, penance is looked upon as a medicinal remedy that can restore the sinner to moral health and social acceptance. McNeill and Gamer summarize this conception of penance well when they write:

> The penitentials offer to the sinner the means of rehabilitation. He is given guidance to the way of recovering harmonious relations with the Church, society, and God. Freed in the process of penance from social censure, he recovers the lost personal values of which his offenses have deprived him. He can once more function as a normal person. Beyond the theological considerations, we see in the detailed prescriptions the objective of an inward moral change, the setting up of a process of character reconstruction which involves the correction of special personal defects and the reintegration of personality.[7]

Contributing to the reason that morality and spirituality were interconnected is that the monk's private confession of sins was done in the context of spiritual guidance. The purpose of confessing sins was to name those actions and attitudes that separated the penitent from God, neighbor, and self. The confession was a step in the process of conversion to restore one's right relationship with God and others. The next step was to do penance, which was for healing and spiritual growth. The task of the monastic confessor was not to judge and impose a sentence of penalties, but to be a compassionate discerner of what heals and helps the penitent to walk again in a way that bespeaks a commitment to the gospel.

But as this monastic spirit waned, penances degenerated from being steps in the process of conversion and healing to becoming acts of atonement for sins viewed as crimes. In time, despite the positive material to be found in the penitentials, the overall impact of their use on the development of moral theology was to leave a legacy of morality's preoccupation with sin and its focus on external deeds. The use of the penitentials implied that the gravity of sin and the depth of conversion from sin could be measured. When we begin to put an emphasis on measurement, then legalism, minimalism, and scrupulosity in the moral and spiritual life are not far behind. The catalog of sins that character-ized the penitentials presented a distorted view of the sinner's rela-tionship to a loving God. They also contributed to moral theology's paying more attention to external deeds (what one did wrong) over the interiority of one's heart and the development of one's character (who one is becoming). Not until we see a con-scious and sustained interest in the interiority of the person, with attention paid to acquiring virtue and forming a strong character, can we again talk about morality converging with spirituality.

Summae Confessorum

The next great genre of literature to influence the development of moral theology and its relation to spirituality was the *summae confessorum*. Although these works first appeared toward the end of the twelfth century, they flourished in response to the discipli-nary decree of Pope Innocent III and the Fourth Lateran Council

(1215) requiring the annual confession of sins. A good confession was an integral confession, that is, all sins had to be confessed along with the circumstances that might change the nature of the sin and the culpability of the penitent. The exacting demands of this legislation called for pastoral handbooks to guide confessors in assuring that penitents made an integral confession of sins. The most famous of these was that of Raymond of Penaforte.

The *summae confessorum* were manuals that gave a list of sins, their classifications, and a set of questions the priest might ask the penitent to ensure interior contrition and an integral confession, as well as to discern what kind of advice to give. According to Killian McDonnell, the emphasis in these *summae* on the integrity of the confession is not just a legalistic compulsion but an opportunity for the confessor to act as a spiritual director to "lure the penitent to God" and into the fullness of the gospel.[8] In this way, they were not totally void of a connection to the spiritual life of the penitent. However, this dimension was not the characterizing feature of these books. According to John Gallagher, while these *summae* were more theological than the Celtic penitentials and provided a compendium of the canonical and theological achievements of their time, they were as sin-centered and law-oriented in their approach to the moral life as the penitentials.[9]

The epoch-making *Decretum* of Gratian (1140) had a significant influence on the juridical tone and character of these *summae*. The *Decretum* reflected the new science of canon law to instill in the confessor the legal sophistication of making distinctions and classifications (such as distinguishing mortal and venial sins). The *summae*, in fact, functioned to put the priests in touch with the laws of the church, the new legal insistence on conforming to fixed laws, and the canonical principles of interpretation.[10] Such a heavy juridical character of the *summae* contributed to further separating morality from spirituality.

The early Scholasticism of the twelfth century also laid the groundwork for separating theology and spirituality. In the twelfth century, Peter Lombard introduced a new method into theological investigation, and the format, method, and distinctions in his collection of *Sentences* (a survey of opinions of theologians and the Fathers of the Church) became the preferred way of studying theology. Substituting questions and answers for the *lectio divina* of monastic theology, the *Sentences* used Aristotle's logic as a method for making distinctions and drawing conclusions. As theology sought more and more a logical framework for understanding and expressing faith, the preoccupation with rational distinctions kept the intellect and will in separate spheres. As a result, theological reflection became more isolated from spirituality and contributed to reducing spirituality to purely religious sentiment. In such a climate, theology and spirituality began to go their separate ways.

According to Philip Sheldrake, several internal developments in spirituality from the twelfth century onward moved spirituality in a new direction. One was the influence of the scholars of the School of St. Victor, especially Richard, who gave special treatment to spirituality by retrieving the mystical theology of Pseudo-Dionysius and making it the measuring rod for the spiritual life. Another development was the increased interest in subjective, affective mystical experiences and the literature generated by it, such as Saint Bernard's commentary on the Song of Songs, which gave expression to spiritual intimacy. A third development was the gradual systematization of meditation and prayer that gave rise to the spiritual renewal in Germany and the Low Countries known as *devotio moderna* with its literature on the "science" of meditation and structured prayer.[11] This New Devotion rejected the idea that one had to be a professional religious person in the monastery or convent in order to live a spiritual life. This movement was inspired by the idea that living in the world was not incompatible with living a spiritual life if one shaped one's life around a meditation on the life of Christ. From this period, we got the spiritual classic of Thomas à Kempis, *The Imitation of Christ*.

Bonaventure and Aquinas provide a brief interlude in which theology is interjected with spirituality. Even though they differed in their approaches to theology, nothing made sense to them apart from its relation to God. Bonaventure was more affective and mystical, focusing on love as the central description of holiness, while Aquinas was more intellectual and analytical, emphasizing truth and acquiring knowledge of truth as the way to holiness. But a separate spirituality and theology had no purpose in the work of either theologian. Nonetheless, the divisions of Aquinas's *Summa*, meant to be a unified work, effectively established the classical scholastic separation of theology into dogmatic and moral theology. Because Thomas placed the subject matter of spirituality in part II (on the virtues), thus making it a subdivision of moral theology, that is where it remained until the present time.

Later, during the Renaissance, the medieval synthesis of an integrated vision of theology broke down more completely. Philip Sheldrake describes the approach to spirituality by the end of the Middle Ages as one marked by separation and divisions. Affective experiences of God were separated from an intellectual understanding of faith to separate spirituality from theology. Morality became further isolated from spirituality by limiting the interest of spirituality to the interior life. As spirituality developed a more focused interest in prayer, contemplation, and mystical experience, it got further removed from ordinary life and became reserved for professional religious people who sought the "higher" way of perfection.[12]

By the end of the sixteenth century, theology in the universities and then later in the seminaries was subdivided into separate disciplines. Over and against Scholastic speculative theology stood mystical and moral theology. Yves Congar notes in his *A History of Theology* that when the spiritual works of Ignatius, Teresa, John of the Cross, Jane Frances de Chantal, and Francis de Sales appeared, they developed from a discipline separate from classical speculative theology.[13] They wrote in terms quite separate from classic theology and developed the new specialty of "spiritual" or "mystical" theology with its own specialized language, style, and sources—namely, their own religious experience or the knowledge they acquired of the interior life from spiritual direction. Yet, when these writers made their presuppositions explicit, they did so in the categories of Scholastic theology.

The Manuals

In the aftermath of the Reformation, the church took up a defensive posture. The Council of Trent (1545–1563) sought to provide clear lines that would distinguish Protestant protest from Catholic orthodoxy. Two reforms of the Council of Trent affected the development of moral theology as a separate theological discipline in Catholic theology. One was the legislation on the sacrament of penance; the other was the establishment of the seminary system. A new theological genre for morality, the *Institutiones theologiae moralis* or the manuals of moral theology, served as the major seminary resource for educating priests in their practical ministry, which was largely a sacramental ministry.

The moral manuals were oriented toward confessional practice. The moral training they provided was heavily concerned with sinfulness and degrees of culpability. The functional relationship between the sacrament of penance and moral theology slanted the whole view of morality for centuries to come, for example, by confining moral thinking to acts penitents were expected to confess and that priests were expected to interpret both for the kind of sin they were and for the degree of guilt the penitent might have in committing them. Immorality, moreover, became focused almost exclusively on actions rather than on the deteriorating dispositions of character.

The Fourth Lateran Council had already turned the spiritual practice of the confession of sins into an ecclesiastical legal obligation. The Council of Trent reinforced that decree with its more extensive treatment of penance in response to the positions of the reformers. In this defensive ecclesial atmosphere, "hearing confessions" became less a service of healing by a "doctor of the soul," as in the earlier monastic practice, and more a judicial act by the priest acting as a "judge" to determine whether the penitent deserved absolution. The juridical character to the sacrament put a great emphasis on an integral confession that required a detailed list of sins, their number, kind, and the circumstances that might change their nature. The very name of the sacrament after this time as *confession* indicates the prominence of this aspect.

To carry out their function as judge well, confessors had to be better trained in matters of the law, the analysis of moral acts, and in distinctions and degrees of sinfulness. The seminary system provided the context for this training. In fact, Catholic moral theology following Trent became, until Vatican II, largely something canon lawyers often taught and that only priests needed to know. The moral manuals were professional books oriented toward aiding the priest in the right exercise of his pastoral ministry, especially as a confessor. This made them more like law books than books of edification or inspiration for living in the world of grace revealed in Jesus Christ. For example, consider the manual of the Jesuit Thomas Slater from 1908, the first to be published in English. In the preface he defined the limits, the scope, and the aim of his work.

> Here, however, we must ask the reader to bear in mind that manuals of moral theology are technical works intended to help the confessor and the parish priest in the discharge of his duties. They are as technical as the text-books of the lawyer and the doctor.

> They are not intended for edification, nor do they
> hold up a high ideal of Christian perfection for the
> imitation of the faithful. They deal with what is of
> obligation under the pain of sin; they are books of
> moral pathology. They are necessary for the Catholic
> priest to enable him to administer the sacrament of
> Penance and to fulfill his other duties....[14]

Slater goes on to say that ascetical literature should be consulted by those who wish to know the ideals of the Christian life that the church encourages (but does not require) people to practice.[15] Even as recently as 1958, the moral compendium of the influential John C. Ford and Gerald Kelly reiterates the principal goal of moral theology to be the forming of confessors to determine the limits of sin and to educate consciences in the sacrament of penance.[16]

There is not enough space here to do justice to all the issues and nuances of the manuals pertaining to the relationship of spirituality and morality. Some, like the work of Saint Alphonsus Liguori, showed a greater sense of integration of morality and spirituality than others. However, an undeniable characteristic of the manualist era as a whole is the attention to actions and the breaking of rules rather than to character and its development or deterioration. Penitents were to confess what they were doing, not the sort of person they were becoming. The prominence given to what constituted a valid celebration of the sacraments in Catholic piety, especially penance and Eucharist, contributed to the juridical interest in moral matters apart from their relation to moral character or to how the moral life might be illumined by the great mysteries of faith or the parts of the Bible that do not deal specifically with law.

Casuistry with the law gave the impression that living within the limits of the law, not the tendencies of one's character, is what the Christian moral life is all about. The challenge to the moral life put forth by the manuals, then, was to discover the appropriate law for each situation and to assess its binding force in the circumstances. Consider, for example, this description of moral theology found in the fifth edition of the English manual of Henry Davis:

> It must be admitted, however, that the science [of moral theology] cannot be anything but juristic. There is a body of law, Divine, Natural, Ecclesiastical and Civil, which has to be explained....A sane legalism, as a sane casuistry, will determine the reasonable and necessary implications of all law, and it is precisely about law that Moral Theology is concerned. It is not a mirror of perfection, showing man the way of perfection.[17]

No wonder that moral theology became more closely aligned with canon law than with spirituality.

With the division of theology into different disciplines, moral theology became further isolated from the influence of scripture, doctrine, and spirituality. When describing the relation of moral theology to spiritual theology, Henry Davis writes this: "Since these two parts of Theology [ascetical and mystical theology] deal with perfection, it would seem better that they should not be formally included in any treatment of Moral Theology as such."[18]

Manuals also appeared in spiritual, or ascetical, theology. Pierre Pourrat's influential *Christian Spirituality*, the first comprehensive history of spirituality, distinguishes morality from spirituality by limiting morality to avoiding sin and spirituality to aiming at perfection through the practice of the virtues by those choosing to aspire to a higher state.[19] *The Spiritual Life: A Treatise on Ascetical and Mystical Theology* by Adolphe Tanquerey, the French Sulpician professor of dogmatic and moral theology at St. Mary's Seminary in Baltimore at the turn of the twentieth century, was widely used from 1930 until the Second Vatican Council. It represents the tradition of restricting morality to what is obligatory and spirituality to what is additional, that is, what may be chosen if one wants to attain perfection, but it is not required of everyone. The proper object of spiritual theology for him is the perfection of the Christian life through virtue.

> It differs from Moral Theology, because, while it presents to our consideration the commandments of God and of the Church, which are the bases of all spiritual life, it insists also on the evangelical counsels, and on a higher degree of virtue than is strictly obligatory. Ascetical Theology, then, is truly *the science of Christian perfection*.[20]

Joseph de Guibert held a similar view that made spirituality stand alongside morality as pertaining to virtuous acts that are above and beyond moral duty and that led to the fullness of Christian life.[21]

The way for the remarriage of spirituality and morality began prior to Vatican II with writers such as Louis Bouyer, who moved away from the style of the manuals to highlight the evangelical foundation of spirituality. Bouyer also saw that morality had to do with more than obligations and so overlapped with spirituality in its concern with the ideal of perfection in the human search for God. For Bouyer, spirituality is located within the heart of morality and not alongside it, even though spirituality's particular concern is with religious exercises and religious experiences, that is, those dimensions of human life where the reference to God is explicit.[22]

During this time of the divorce of morality and spirituality, the moral and spiritual aspects of life were not so radically separated as to have nothing to do with each other in practice. On the one hand, from within the arena of moral theology, for example, the excessively legal mentality and the juridical model of confession were softened by integrating the moral and spiritual concerns of the penitent in the actual practice of confession. The confessor was not merely to distinguish the licit from the illicit but he was also to respond to the human hunger for growing in the spiritual life. Ford and Kelly instruct in their manual that good confessors must pay attention to the spiritual dimensions of the penitent's life and not merely to moral guilt.[23] On the other hand, from within spirituality, the moral and spiritual aspects of life were kept together in the devotional literature that grew in reaction to the speculative intricacies of medieval spirituality directed toward mystical experience. From the fourteenth-century *devotio moderna*, with its affective type of spirituality answering to the practical needs of devout Christians, through the humanism of the sixteenth and seventeenth centuries in such figures as Erasmus and Francis de Sales, the focus turns to the virtuous response to meeting Christ in the Bible. One first hears the call of God through scripture and then responds. In such an approach, the spiritual life gives birth to the moral life.[24]

However, there was a significant consequence of keeping morality divorced from spirituality. According to John Mahoney, the legal focus of the manuals led moral theology to relinquish to spiritual theology an interest in becoming a good person. But, as Mahoney goes on to show, spiritual theology unfortunately pursued this interest in an elitist atmosphere more suited for those called to a special holiness apart from the world, particularly those in cloistered religious orders, rather than for the laity who were to live ordinary lives of faith. Even when the manuals adopted the schema of the virtues rather than the commandments, these were often seen as remedies for sin or as a new measure for determining sin.[25] Michael Downey shows that as long as spirituality pertained to the interior life, the life of perfection, or to the mystical graces which were the prerogative of a few, then it became further removed from what was thought necessary for Christian living, namely, obeying the commandments and participating in the sacraments. "Spirituality" came to be understood in contradistinction to "the world of devotions" where the life of virtue was located and expressed.[26]

But the separation of morality from spirituality went deeper than method and content. It was, at its core, a divorce of thought from feeling. That deep division suggested two paths to God—the journey of the heart through love, prayer, and action, and the journey of the mind through knowledge, understanding, and theory. Morality lost touch with the role of the emotions and the imagination in the moral life and took on a too-exclusive emphasis on the intellect and will. The wedge driven between feeling and thought eclipsed the spiritual experience entailing both mind and heart that ultimately lies at the depths of the moral life. Only in recent years of renewal has morality both retrieved the initiating experience of God's call or offer of love as its spiritual core and raised to greater prominence the roles of emotion and imagination in the moral life.

Remarriage

John Gallagher's judgment rings true that just as the theological, cultural, and pastoral concerns surrounding the Council of Trent occasioned the rise of manualist theology, so new theological, cultural, and pastoral needs provided the catalyst for the Second Vatican Council and occasioned the demise of manualist theology.[27] The manualist era of theology left us a vision of spirituality that was too theoretical, elitist, otherworldly, and individualistic.[28] It left us a vision of moral theology that was too focused on the individual, one-sidedly confession-oriented in its preoccupation with exterior acts as sins, obsessed with the law, and seminary controlled.[29] A fair criticism of each of these disciplines as they came to us on the eve of the Second Vatican Council is that they were too narrow in scope and purpose. Moral theology needed to be transformed from a discipline for confessors to one of critical understanding of faith for Christian living. Spirituality needed to be transformed from its elitist, otherworldly concerns to something more holistic, experiential, and accessible to all. For this to happen, moral theology and spirituality would have to be more informed by the Word, integrated with the great mysteries of faith, and rooted in the experience of the people.

According to Michael Downey, the contemporary renewal in spirituality has been prompted and shaped by three orientations of the Second Vatican Council: the universal call to holiness, the centrality of scripture in the Christian's life and prayer, and the importance of liturgy, especially the Eucharist.[30] The renewal of moral theology has been directed by the council's call that it be more thoroughly informed by scripture and integrated with the great mysteries of faith.

The challenge to enrich moral theology with teaching drawn from scripture and to integrate it with spirituality and the great mysteries of faith had already begun prior to the Council. Emile Mersch, for example, based morality on the notion of the mystical body (1937),[31] and Gerard Gilleman put love at the center of the moral life in his major book of moral reform, *The Primacy of Charity in Moral Theology* (1952).[32] Fritz Tillman offered discipleship of Christ as the overarching framework for morality in *The Master Calls* (1960).[33] However, the most significant work for the renewal movement was Bernard Haring's *The Law of Christ* (1954).[34]

Few works were as popular as Haring's, and no one contributed more to the general spirit of renewal in moral theology and the integration of morality and spirituality than he did. His "charter document" of renewal in moral theology retained an interest in the concerns of the manuals while reconstructing moral theology based on the spiritual response to the call of God in Christ and through the Spirit. Haring replaced the legalistic, sin-oriented approach to the moral life with a vision of morality as the response to the movement of the Spirit in our lives. The "call-response" structure of the moral life and the centrality of the themes of conversion and discipleship in moral theology made it possible to overcome the artificial distinction between morality and spirituality and to remove the double standard of Christian living whereby the commandments and counsels were to be realized by the laity and religious respectively. After Haring's work, there has been no turning back on his major thesis that morality is the response to the spiritual experience of God's enabling love. In that key insight morality and spirituality are inseparably intertwined.

A renewed moral theology has experienced a shift from action to agent and from external law to the inner presence of the Holy Spirit. Morality's primary concern is no longer on mere actions (the right things to do) but also and more fundamentally on the character of the human agent (the sort of person one should be). Moreover, morality is emphasizing today that our ultimate guide to goodness is not found in obedience to external laws but in the discerning heart guided by the Holy Spirit in search of what contributes to the well-being of all. Spirituality and morality exist in a critical-dialogical relationship with one another. Their interests inevitably overlap.

THE CALL TO HOLINESS

A renewed morality is coming to realize its spiritual core, and a renewed spirituality is realizing that it cannot be separate from a way of life. Through spirituality, we pay attention to the depth dimensions of human life. Through morality we pay attention to the public face of that spiritual depth. In short, spirituality and morality show two levels of concern in the one human experience of God. The fruits of one's spirituality are in the moral life, and the roots of one's moral life are in one's spirituality. Spirituality gives rise to moral living, and one's moral life then tests the authenticity of one's experience of God and one's convictions about the way life ought to be.

PART II

❖

Uncovering the Foundations

3.

Being Human Before God

❖

The first two chapters showed that one's Christian spirituality arises from a personal experience of God and that morality expresses our response to God. Spirituality and the moral life are linked by this common term of reference—an experience of God. Without attempting a complete anthropology, this chapter turns to the subject of that experience, the human person, with the question, "What is it about being human that makes it possible to experience God and to live in response to God?" Chapter 4 will examine the experience of God.

Some aspects of being human are especially significant for making the connections between spirituality and morality. The ever-familiar distinction between body and soul that we inherited from the Greek philosophical tradition helps us to appreciate both embodiment and spirituality as important aspects of who we are. However, a too neat separation of body and soul has only caused havoc in our spiritual tradition. In chapter 1, the models of spirituality represented by Simeon Stylites and Sally Mae show what can happen when we subordinate the body and our experiences of the world and human relationships to the "higher" realm of the spirit and make spirituality primarily a matter of "the interior life" of caring for the soul. The understanding of spirituality and morality in this book calls for a holistic view of the person as a psychosomatic unity. For that purpose, a biblically grounded anthropology is more conducive than the Greek model.[1]

In 1 Thessalonians 5:23, Paul lines up three aspects of a biblical anthropology: "May the God of peace himself sanctify you entirely; and may your spirit and soul and body be kept sound and blameless at the coming of our Lord Jesus Christ." Each term, spirit (*pneuma*), soul (*psyche*), and body (*soma*), does not denote a "part" of the person so that we end up with three opposing parts. Rather, understanding being human before God through these aspects is like looking at the person through a kaleidoscope. Each turn of the lens offers another view of a multifaceted reality. In a biblical anthropology, each term refers to the whole person but from a different perspective. As in the saying "All hands on deck," a part is used to stand for the whole. The reference to a part (hands) calls attention to a characteristic of the whole (sailors called to do manual labor).

While these biblical anthropological terms certainly can and do, at times, refer to particular features alone (*spirit* can mean "breath" and *soul* does not include body parts in its meaning), they are often used to refer to the whole person from a particular view.[2] "Spirit" highlights the self with the deep desire or holy longing to be fulfilled as an authentic person. It is the very root of the spiritual and moral life. "Soul" is not the immaterial principle of Greek philosophy, but the heart-center that makes each person uniquely original. Emotion and imagination are its instruments for connecting spirit to body. "Body" is a view of the person from the outside, as it were. It gives physical expression to our spirit and soul. Through the body, we experience the world and express our relationship to God, to others, and to the world. A richer appreciation of being human before God comes as we harmonize the fuller constellation of meaning from each of these perspectives on the person.

Spirit

"Spirit" has roots in the concrete notion of *ruah*, wind or breath. In the Old Testament we learn that God's breath is the creative power of life. Bodies come alive when God breathes forth into them (Gen 2:7; Ezek 37:6–10). The human spirit is not something the body generates by itself. Even when the bones, muscle, and skin come together in Ezekiel 37's vision of reviving dry bones, God must confer the spirit before the body comes alive. When the body dies and returns to dust, the spirit returns to God (Ps 104:29–30; Job 34:14). Life and death depend on this vital power coming from God and returning to God. The spirit is God's life within humans, empowering them to reason, to choose, and to act. In short, the spirit puts humans in dynamic relationship with God and enables them to do what they were created to do.[3]

The New Testament also sees the spirit as something given to us by God (Rom 8:15; 1 Cor 2:12). The same spirit that animated Jesus now animates us. Jesus "breathed out" his spirit on all through his death and resurrection (John 19:30). For Paul, we live with, in, and through the power of the same spirit as

Jesus (1 Cor 6:17; Rom 5:5; Gal 2:20). From this biblical perspective on "spirit," we see that to be human can only rightly be understood in light of God's taking the initiative to breathe into us this animating power. To be human as spirit is first to be more gift than achievement, since it is God's animating breath that gives us life. To be human as spirit means that our inmost nature is desire. We are by nature a longing desire for the God by whom we live, which we may experience as a longing for wholeness, happiness, fulfillment, or meaning.

The spiritual journey begins out of this holy longing. "Do you love me?" is a universal, persistent human quest. As spirit, we are creatures of a deep desire to love, to be loved, and to move toward union with the source of all love. Spiritualities of any sort try to satisfy this deep longing by providing a way to integrate the fragments of our life into a meaningful whole around the love that ultimately satisfies. This longing for loving union with that which gives ultimate value is what the human spirit (and "spirituality" for that matter) is all about. It is what makes us "spiritual" by nature.

Theistic faith sees this restless longing as an amazing grace. We are born with this ravenous hunger to be whole, to be in communion with what gives us ultimate value—what believers call God. Our capacity for this loving union is not a human achievement but a gift of God, who has already reached out in love to us. As Saint John reminds us, "In this is love, not that we loved God but that he loved us" (1 John 4:10); and again, "You did not choose me but I chose you" (John 15:16). As the spiritual masters have taught, we would not be searching for God if God had not already found us.

The fact that we are already seeking God at all means that God has planted the seeds of this desire within us, imprinting the Holy Spirit on our spirit to give us a pre-conscious desire for God. It is like the parents who give their children money to buy them a Christmas gift. The children would not be able to show their love for their parents through a simple gift if it weren't for the parents loving them first by giving them money to buy the gift. So it is with spiritual and moral striving. The spiritual and moral life is possible in the first place because God has made the first move. Our whole life is lived in response to the love we first received as a gift of God's graciousness. Our spiritual disciplines are an expression of our desire to surrender completely to God's love for us and our love for God, and our moral life is about living out of the abundance of being loved in ways that make life richer for everyone.

Spirituality and morality, then, begin with this immense desire that is the human spirit haunted by God's Spirit. God is already and always at work opening us to mystery and moving us to seek what ultimately satisfies—union with God. When we realize that the discontent of the human spirit is inspired by God's Spirit, then this "holy nagging" gives way to an invitation or a call to move beyond ourselves and to become more than we are right now. Amazing grace beckons us as it beckoned Moses through the burning bush, Saul on his way to Damascus, or the salesman in this story that I once heard on retreat.

Several years ago a group of computer salesmen from Silicon Valley went to Chicago for a sales convention. They assured their wives that they would be back to the hotel in plenty of time for dinner. But one thing led to another and the meeting ran overtime. As they raced to the El, one man inadvertently kicked over a table supporting a basket of apples. Without stopping, they all reached the train with a sigh of relief. All but one.

This man paused, and felt a twinge of compunction for the boy whose apple stand had been overturned. He waved good-bye to his companions and returned to the apple stand. He was glad he did. The ten-year-old boy was blind. The salesman gathered up the apples and noticed that several of them were bruised. He handed the boy twenty dollars and said, "Take this money for the damage I did. I hope it won't spoil your day." As he started to walk away, the bewildered boy called after him, "Are you Jesus?" He stopped in his tracks. He wondered.

And so it goes. Something or someone makes a claim on us. We get stopped in our tracks and ask ourselves who we are and where we are going.

Theologians see this as an expression of our capacity for self-transcendence. This means that we never have to stay stuck where we are. We have the ability to move beyond the present, to move beyond ourselves by reaching out to others in knowledge, freedom, and love. In so moving, we keep getting closer to "having it all together" in terms of our deepest desire to love and to be loved. For the person of faith, the nagging craving for more is a divine invitation to seek what is genuinely fulfilling. Through our capacity for transcendence we are always on the lookout for the one person, the one job, the one experience, the one position in society, or the one possession that will fulfill us. Our hunger for God gets disguised in these human longings. So we collect things, people, experiences, and sensations and get hijacked along the way by what spiritual writers have called "inordinate" attachments to the world's created goods. Today we call this having an addiction.[4] Although these created goods satisfy many human longings, if only in a passing way, they merely whet our appetite for the fulfillment or happiness that is lasting.

Our deeper hunger is not satisfied even as we grow fat by our consumerist consumption. Just when we think that we have found the one thing that will fulfill us, we discover that it is not enough. When a new BMW tools by our pre-owned Lexus, we suddenly feel poor. That certain amount of wealth and possessions that we thought would satisfy us never does. We want more. But, as we acquire it, even more looms before us. When we seem to have it all (money, fame, health), our spirit is still not quiet. We remain unsatisfied even as our latest acquisition is proudly in our hands. It promises what God promises, but it fails to deliver. As we try to wring from these created goods the satisfaction that can only come from God, we are searching for the right thing but in the wrong place. God remains the "object" of our ultimate concern. Not until we withdraw from addictive behaviors, or from our inordinate attachments, will our deepest desire for love be set free.

THE CALL TO HOLINESS

The immense longing that we feel underscores that nothing finite ultimately satisfies us. "Why am I not happier with all this stuff?" we cry out in protest, but to no one in particular. But such a question that originates in our spiritual nature is one that God cannot resist answering. Our searching for meaning, hungering for love, yearning to connect, and seeking fulfillment are part of the interior dynamic of the human spirit moving us toward union with God. Nothing short of uniting these longings with loving God will ever make us who we are meant to be and satisfy our craving spirit. These inner longings make monks of us all, for they are an implicit call to search for fulfillment in loving God who alone has the goodness and wholeness to satisfy us. We are finally fulfilled and have arrived home at peace to the extent that we share in the goodness of God. Only in God, as Augustine says, do we find the love necessary to end our restlessness.

So this dimension of being human that we call "spirit" makes spirituality and the moral life possible for us, because as "spirit" we have the capacity to receive and to give, to be open to mystery, and to be in relationship with something more than ourselves. As spirit, we are already being drawn to God, but in such a way that we can refuse to follow. Our freedom is engaged but not enslaved by God's love. We can say Yes or No. Without destroying our freedom, God's love for us has so affected the human spirit as to make a claim on us and to give us an orientation toward life and love. God creates us free to be loving or selfish. We can hand ourselves over to grace or to sin. Theologians have named this basic orientation of the self either for or against God as our fundamental option.[5] While the term can be misleading by suggesting that this basic "option" is one more choice alongside others, its value is that it points to a depth dimension of our moral identity or character. The "fundamental option" gives an enduring quality and stable direction to our lives, influences our sense of responsibility to and for our world, and gives personal meaning to our actions in an ultimate way.

We express our fundamental option in and through the everyday choices we make or the habits we form. But we usually do not exhaust it in any of these. Sometimes, we might engage a "great decision," as Bernard Haring would call it,[6] that involves a significant degree of self-awareness and self-possession so as to reaffirm or alter our character. But more often than not, we manifest this depth dimension of our freedom in the way we live everyday morality. To so dispose ourselves to God that we come to love God and to care about what God cares about is both a moral and spiritual task. To strengthen our orientation toward God is a function of spiritual practices as well as the moral practice of virtue.

Soul

The soul integrates spirit and body into a single personal expression. The soul prevents the person from getting lost in the interior world of the spirit's relationship to God and so lose sight of one's relationship to the world; and the soul prevents the person from getting lost in the exterior world of the body's relationship to created reality and so lose sight of one's deeper relationship to God. One of the themes that runs through the writing of a contemporary spiritual mentor, Thomas Moore, is that when people say they are losing their spirituality, they are actually losing touch with their soul that connects their life experiences to their inner spirit.[7] Losing one's spirituality is to starve one's soul by failing to feed it. Soul food is whatever arouses deep feelings and stirs the imagination, for these are the instruments of the soul and the raw material of one's character. What we deeply care about and how we perceive and create our world are the soulful dimensions of our spirituality and morality. We touch a person's soul when we feel the life-giving, energizing, insightful, and creative capacity of the person coming through.

But *soul* eludes precise definition. It is a rich notion with many ways to describe it. In the biblical sense, "soul" is a way to consider the person as if from the inside. The biblical notion of *nephesh* does not involve "having" a soul, as though the soul were an immortal, immaterial entity enclosed in the body that we must save through our spiritual practices. Rather, soul stands for the whole person who receives life (Gen 2:7). As Hans Walter Wolff concludes in his treatment of the soul, it is the "sphere marked out by the stirrings of the mind and the emotions."[8] In other words, when we stand in awe of a snowcapped peak, it is not our bodies or minds that gasp, "Wow!" It's the soul.

The most frequently used notion that expresses the self as soul is "heart" *(leb)*. According to Wolff, *heart* is the "most important" and "commonest" of all anthropological terms in the Old Testament.[9] The heart is the ultimate source of physical, emotional, intellectual, and volitional life. It is the "mission control center" of the moral life. It is the seat of virtue as well as of vice, of faith as well as of doubt, of thinking as well as of feeling. In the recesses of the heart dwell the insights, intentions, desires, memories, fears, and hopes that determine the person's character. From the heart we respond to God's initiative or refuse to do so. No wonder the biblical world sees the heart to be of special concern to God.[10] It may be hidden from others and even from oneself, but God searches its depths and knows it through and through.

The hope of the messianic prophecies is for the people to receive a new heart so that their inmost inclinations will be to live out of divine love in loyalty to the covenant (Jer 31:33; Ezek 11:19 and 36:26). Hearts of stone are unreceptive to God's law, whereas new hearts of flesh are receptive, full of insight, and ready to obey. The prophets Ezekiel and Jeremiah tell us that God's law is written in our heart, so that if we listen to the murmurings of our heart, we will hear the message of God for us.

The Markan summary of Jesus' proclamation of the reign of God is the call for a new heart (Mark 1:15). Jesus continues the tradition of the heart's being the wellspring of the moral life with his concern about the filth on the inside of the cup that shows itself on the outside (Matt 23:25–26). This means that from a person's heart come the evil ideas that lead one to do immoral things (Mark 7:21), whereas a good person produces goodness from the good in the heart (Luke 6:45). The Lukan Jesus aptly summarizes the implications of the unity of the person and the centrality of the heart as the source of action: "For it is out of the abundance of the heart that the mouth speaks" (Luke 6:45).

Living from the heart requires the nurture and discipline of prayer. The practice of turning to God with our eyes and ears rooted in the heart enables us to discern how we might respond to the challenge of God's loving us. Jesus said, "For where your treasure is, there your heart will be also" (Matt 6:21). When our hearts treasure God, all other treasures will be treasured rightly. With the heart so rightly ordered, the good and the holy are inseparable. The spiritual life of holiness and the moral life of virtue walk hand in hand. According to the biblical vision, the rightly ordered heart will have a certain instinct for what is good relative to God. Such a properly ordered heart yields a life of virtue. The misdirected heart produces sin. The rightly ordered heart hears God's call to be our best selves and to do what is right. In such an understanding of the "heart" as this lie the biblical roots for what we today call moral character and conscience, where conscience is not a distinct faculty but a reference for the whole person, who must integrate a range of operations in coming to know moral values and to judge in light of them.

The Reasoning Heart

Given this rich understanding of the heart, how are we to understand "reason"? In giving such a prominent role to the heart, we must guard against the false impression that the biblical self is determined more by feeling than by reason. The real core meaning of *heart* includes everything that we would ascribe to the "head and heart" working together. The aim of life is to have a heart of wisdom (Prov 8:5; 18:15).[11] Having wisdom is related to the practical virtue of prudence, the virtue of the "reasoning heart," the soul in paraphrase.

The "reasoning" that expresses the soul through holiness and virtue is much more than the reasoning we usually identify with ethics. In the history of ethics, two modes of reasoning have been dominant. One, the deontological mode, draws particular conclusions from laws or principles that express moral obligations. The other, the teleological mode, emphasizes the goal, ideal, or value to be realized in the outcome or consequences of one's decision. But do these modes fully define the way we reason morally? The temptation is to reduce the whole of reasoning to "heady" analytical reasoning that would give us absolute objectivity either by a detached process of drawing conclusions from principles or by calculating consequences. Reasoning in ethics, as in science, tries to proceed on the basis of an accurate grasp of what is going on. To do that, it gathers pertinent evidence, sifts out the relevant facts, puts the best evidence in a logical sequence, draws a conclusion, and tests the results. After all, our moral values are ultimately grounded in reality. But philosophers tell us that no one, not even the scientist, can be an "ideal observer" or an "impartial spectator" with absolute objectivity.

The reasoning of the soul is not limited to a purely intellectual activity. The moral and spiritual life cannot go forward with heartless head in command. The soul's "reasoning heart" knows this because it integrates head and heart. Our affective connection and imaginative immersion in the realities of the moral order illumine aspects we would otherwise miss. How else do we know which facts are morally relevant, which principles to use, which consequences count? In these decisions there is not just the scientist at work; there is also the mystic. Ethical reasoning is bound up with feelings, intuitions, the imagination, as well as a sense of the fitting. In this way, the reasoning heart aligns itself closely to the character of the moral agent and to the art form of the spiritual practice of the discernment of spirits. This is more than a linear sequence of stepwise logical procedures. Around the flow of discursive reasoning, moral discernment engages affective sensibilities and experienced perceptions of the imagination that enable us to interpret what is going on and to order priorities. The instruments of the soul that animate the discernment of the reasoning heart are the emotions and the imagination.

Emotion

The moral life is the child of our affections. The spiritual source of our actions is the heart moved by love, as in this scene told by John Shea:

> There is a story about a busy man who one day hurriedly headed out the door for work. In his path was his three-year-old son playing with blocks. The man patted the boy on the head, stepped over him, opened the door, and went outside. Halfway down the walk a guilt bomb exploded inside him.
>
> "What am I doing?" he thought to himself. "I am ignoring my son. I never play with him. He'll be old before I know it."...
>
> He returned to the house and sat down with his son and began to build blocks. After two minutes, the boy said, "Daddy why are you mad at me?"[12]

Shea goes on to show that the quality and effectiveness of our actions is affected not only by what we do, but also by the spiritual source of our actions that is deeper than our motivation, which can be too much a matter of the mind. Just doing the right thing is not enough to be moral. Being moral also involves feeling the appropriate emotions. As Shea says, "Playing blocks out of guilt is not the same as playing blocks out of love, and the difference is quickly spotted."[13]

Morality has missed its connection to spirituality and the spiritual source of actions because we have approached the moral life from the neck up. We have been too quick to make moral judgments merely a matter of reason. We glory in analysis. We design our interventions, size up the pluses and minuses, marshal our skills, act, evaluate, analyze again, and revise our strategies if necessary according to the outcome. Such moral calculations dissociate moral reasoning from feelings and from the body as much as possible. We deprive the moral life of its affective component and moral reasoning of emotional content. To raise one's voice for the place of emotion in the moral life in such a rationalistic context may be nothing more than a hiccup in a hurricane. But to exalt moral reasoning to the exclusion of emotion is to risk overlooking the state of one's soul. Actions always come from someplace inside us. What we feel emotionally greatly influences what we do and the quality of our actions.

In the history of spirituality, our tradition has a blemished record of positive regard for the emotions. The negative evaluation of concupiscence has stigmatized the affective side of personal life. Feelings have been approached selectively, with ascetical practices developed to help us control some (like anger and sexual feelings) and to cultivate others (like reverence, compassion, sorrow). One strain of the tradition coming from the Greek patristic authors advocated an indifference to, or freedom from, the emotions by turning to God through contemplation of truths. Western authors acknowledged some role for feelings, and wanted to control them rather than eliminate them. Benedict, Bernard of Clairvaux, Aquinas and Bonaventure, Francis de Sales and Ignatius have a positive appreciation for feelings and how they can lead to a deeper relationship with God and others. Contemporary spirituality has partnered with psychology in appreciating the role of feelings in spiritual growth.[14]

To retrieve the affective dimension of the moral life is to reclaim its mystical side. *Mystical* is a perfectly apt word, but it has acquired the unfortunate connotation of being a rare, strange experience of specialists. This is a pity. The mystical refers to the affective dimension of our lives. Moral awareness, in fact, is born in the mystical. That is to say, we enter the moral enterprise of reflection, argument, and responsible living through an affective grasp of the worth of persons and the web of relationships with others and the environment in which we live.[15] To assess the full import of what it means to be moral, then, we must include the mystical capacity of the human soul expressed through the emotions.[16]

Emotions are evaluative perceptions, not neutral outbursts. Sidney Callahan and Charles Shelton, two psychologists interested in morality, have written on behalf of bringing emotion back into our discussion of what constitutes a moral response. They argue that emotions contain some element of judgment, for they are produced by the immediate, initial, and implicit cognitive estimate that we make of the qualitative features of our experience.[17] In this way they are like antennae seeking the first signs of moral life outside ourselves. We enter the arena of moral reasoning through the doorway of an emotional response to people and events. How we are moved stimulates critical reflection and makes us lean toward acting in certain ways. Because of our emotional dispositions, we perceive certain features of a situation to be morally significant and form an evaluative attitude toward them. That is why we can say that, at the most general level, we feel and intuit, immediately and without argument, a sense of attraction or revulsion by something that seems right or wrong about things we hold dear. For example, the sense of excitement and relief that we feel when we see someone protected from harm by another or rescued from a natural disaster is an "ethics attack": "Yes, that's the way we ought to be." We are affectively attracted to those kinds of people and those sorts of actions that defend life and liberty or display honesty and courage, for these values express what it means to be human and to be community. So, too, the revulsion we feel when we look at another news clip of the atrocities of war is an "ethics attack" crying out for a remedy, a vision or standard of what ought to be so as to change this horrible situation. We are driven to get our rational analysis straight because we feel deeply about the values at stake and are already involved in a preliminary, precritical appraisal of what our responsibility ought to be.

Timothy O'Connell has shown that our moral tradition has not been totally void of including the role of feelings in the

81

moral life. In this tradition, we spoke of this "ethics attack" as the evaluative knowledge that we need in order to make a moral choice. Evaluative knowledge is heart knowledge. It is the felt knowledge that we have when we are "caught up" in someone or something through personal involvement and reflection. With evaluative knowledge we appreciate affectively the qualitative dimensions of a situation. So the moral awareness that leads to action is a mix of affective and conceptual knowledge, head and heart. We feel as well as know what is right or wrong.[18]

Rationalists will raise a suspicious eyebrow at the thought of giving a place to emotions, and they will never fail to remind us that emotions are more often founts of fallacy than wells of wisdom. Emotions can be wrong about the full moral import of a situation. For rationalists, nothing fogs the mind or clouds our judgment quite like emotion. To be objective, they say, is to be detached; to be careful in deliberation is to be cool, calm, and collected. If we get emotionally involved, they fear, we will not be able to see the truth of our situation. That may be so up to a point. After all, our emotions are a two-edged sword. On the one hand, they provide knowledge and evaluation of our moral concerns; on the other hand, they have the potential to distort our moral response. They are subject to social conditioning and need to be tested against broader experience and critical reflection. To seek the truth only by means of the emotions, unaided by critical reflection, is blindly prejudicial and can lead to chaos.[19]

But distance and detachment do not always help us see clearly. Emotions can provide a cognitive window on the world.

Even though we strive to shape our conduct around considerations of reason, reason is not the sole arbiter of our moral commitments. Through the emotions we come to know the truth of an event in its subtlety and totality. We notice through feelings what we might otherwise miss by a detached intellect.[20] For example, a mother's love for her child alerts her to even slight changes in her child that detachment would never see. Likewise, the emotional pain of losing a parent, a spouse, or a child does not distract us from the truth of their death but helps us perceive this loss in its fullness. Similarly, the truth of the social reality of the unemployed, the homeless, or the medically uninsured cannot be conveyed merely by statistics but more accurately by the stories these people tell of their anguish and despair.

If we were to remain chained to discursive reason and conceptual knowledge as the only valid forms of knowing in matters of spirituality and morality, then God and moral truth would not touch us. Emotions awaken insight. Philosopher Paul Ricoeur affirms as much when he says that feelings bind together what knowledge divides and sets over against us, and feelings bring us into a closer bond with the other than conceptual knowledge does.[21] The moralist Daniel Maguire and psychologists Sidney Callahan and Charles Shelton suggest the same when they argue that feelings are not neutral but evaluative reactions. Affective knowing is genuine knowledge that calls for completion in the conceptual, analytic form of knowing.[22]

This insight about the relation of emotion to moral knowledge opens a way for us to understand how it is that differences in moral judgments are often rooted in different spiritualities.

The affective dimension of ourselves is the soulful connection linking morality to spirituality. While the language of principles and consequences that make up our public discourse is the product of cognitive reflection, such reflection is a step removed from our heart-center and the true expression of who we are and what we stand for. Clearer indicators of the soul come through feelings, intuitions, and somatic reactions. Although morality has for too long neglected these prereflective sources as reliable guides to moral truth, our spiritual tradition of discernment has relied on them as pathways for discovering what is fitting.

We often come to an impasse in moral discussions not because one of us favors principles and another consequences. We disagree because our hearts are not in the same place. Consider again the case of T.K. from the Introduction. Where we stand morally on treatment, comfort care only, or euthanasia is primarily a matter of "where we are" in our heart-center, that is, emotionally and imaginatively. After all, our choices of value are affective appreciations of value. When our hearts are not in the same place, we will not see the same things and we will not care about the same values, or at least not to the same degree. Our tradition of discernment reminds us that the murmurings of the heart are the messages of God. Moral judgments that arise from listening to these heart murmurs are judgments made in response to what we ultimately love, to what deeply motivates us, to what gives us meaning and identity. We disagree on moral matters ultimately because we differ at the level of soul where our spirituality informs our morality.

Sometimes theologians talk about this affective moral awareness as connatural knowledge, the knowledge of one whose heart is attuned to the good because of acquired virtue.[23] Connatural knowledge reminds us that, while we can reach a correct judgment intellectually by the right use of reason, there is also another way. It is by way of the affections determining what is reasonable. One who is good knows the morally good by a felt resonance between one's own being and the act to be done. This incident demonstrates it concretely:

> When I was seven I had to have my tonsils removed. The operation was scheduled for early in the morning, and I was forbidden to have any food or drink after dinner the evening before. The operation was delayed, and I recall lying for several hours on a surgical bed in a corridor outside the operating room. My mouth was so dry that I couldn't swallow. My lips were so parched they hurt.
>
> There I was, a child all alone, sobbing and begging for a glass of water. Every now and then a nurse passed by, saw me crying, explained why I couldn't have a drink, and went back to work. Then one nurse I had not seen before stopped and asked if she could help. Again I pleaded for water. Like the others, she explained that she couldn't give me anything to drink, but then she did something totally unexpected: She told me that her lips were moist with lipstick and that maybe a kiss would make my lips moist, too. She bent

> down, kissed me, wished me well, and went back to her work....
>
> I don't remember if her kiss made my thirst go away, but I do know it made my loneliness go away. It was a kiss that spoke volumes about the ties of love that bind us—better than a thousand Sunday sermons.[24]

How did this Good Samaritan nurse know that moist lips kissing parched lips was the right thing to do? No nursing manual prescribes it. How did she know? She knew by heart. That's connatural knowledge.

Theologians who are retrieving virtue tell us that affective connatural knowing is the normal way a good person knows what to do. It is not an alternative system for when discursive reason fails. When we are unable to rely on our ability to discern connaturally, then we have to turn to reasoning from moral principles and consequences.

But we cannot really talk about making this soulful connection to moral living until we have the capacity for an affective experience of the value of persons. To be moral and to be loving imply one another. Research on the role of empathy shows how important this human feeling is in the development of the moral conscience.[25] Empathy first requires sensitivity to what is different from us in another and what is the same. It is an affective and imaginative capacity to cross over into another's experience, identify with the pains and pleasures of the other, and then return to one's self. When empathy is born, care is born, and with it morality. To be morally good we must be able to go out of ourselves and put ourselves in the place of another and of many others, and then come back to our own sense of self.

There are individuals who are so limited in their emotional capacity, perhaps because they have been deprived or abused at a time when they should have been nurtured, that their sensitivity to another and interest in being moral are negligible. Acquiring the capacity for empathy requires the proper environment, especially in our early years, if it is ever to emerge in full power as part of the conscience of an adult. The "cold-blooded killer" murders with no feeling for the victim. What is missing in a psychopath is not the knowledge of right or wrong, but the sensitivity to another and the caring commitment to do the right thing. The psychopath has no empathy. To pour ourselves into what we do requires an emotional capacity to care about others and to commit ourselves to ideals and standards. One of the most common difficulties with those of us who are not psychopaths is not that we do not know what is right, but that we are too lazy to care enough to want to do it. The great enemy of moral and spiritual growth is apathy (from the Greek for "passionless" or "without feeling"). It is what the biblical writers called a "hard heart." That is, we have a loss of care, desire, or passion for doing the right thing and for becoming a good person. Without a commitment of the heart, we will not seek to be good or to do what is right. This is what led psychologist Sidney Callahan to warn that we should "be especially aware that graver moral danger arises from a deficit of moral emotion than from emotional excess."[26]

Contrast these two stories of apathy and care, of being without soul and being soulful. The first depicts what can happen when we live without soul because our passion for justice has been so deadened that atrocities connected to violence are no longer felt as a problem. It is from the film *The River's Edge*. The story line of the film is taken from a true incident in California when a teenaged boy kills his girlfriend for no apparent reason and then leaves her lying by the river's edge. He returns to town and brags to his buddies about what he has done. He invites them to go down to the river's edge and look at the dead body. They go, look, and then return home. No one does anything about it. No one calls the police, the girl's parents, or even their own parents. Nothing. Why? The movie explores the root of violence in the moral numbness of society. These teens are alienated from their emotions and from their moral values. They show no empathy, no caring, only apathy. They look at the girl's dead body and then carry on with life as usual. They have no spiritual source for action. They see an act of injustice and are not moved by it. This is a sign of stunted moral character. They have lost their soul.

By contrast, there is the story told by John Shea of a woman who took her aging mother into her home. The mother had a stroke and needed time to recover. The daughter was painstakingly attentive to her mother's every need, yet a fight broke out over a hard-boiled egg. "Why are you doing all this for me anyway?" asked the mother. The daughter began to list her reasons:

> I was afraid for her; I wanted her to get well; I felt maybe I'd ignored her when I was younger; I needed to show her I was strong; I needed to get her ready for going home alone; old age; and on and on. I was

amazed myself. I could have gone on giving reasons all night. Even she was impressed.

"Junk," she said when I was done.

"Junk?" I yelled. Like, boy, she'd made a real mistake with that remark. I could really get her.

"Yes, junk," she said again, but a little more quietly. And that little-more-quietly tone got to me. And she went on: "You don't have to have all those reasons. We love each other. That's enough."

I felt like a child again. Having your parents show you something that's true, but you don't feel put down — you feel better, because it is true, and you know it. I said, "You're right. You're really right. I'm sorry." She said, "Don't be sorry. Junk is fine. It's what we don't need anymore. I love you."[27]

Shea goes on to show that love is the spiritual source of the woman's actions. The soulful place of love is far deeper than the reasons the daughter gives for what she is doing. The place of love in the soul makes all the reasons of the mind look like junk. Reasons or motives are one thing, but acting soulfully is quite another. It is like Thomas More's reply to his daughter Margaret in Robert Bolt's play, *A Man for All Seasons*. After Margaret has made an emotional plea to her father that he has done all that God can reasonably want of him, Thomas More sees through the reasons of her mind into her heart and replies, "Well...finally...it isn't a matter of reason; finally it's a matter of love."[28] Those who live with soul know the truth of that remark.

Living morally from the heart-center is more than the sum of reasons for doing what is right. There is a soulful, affective component to it as well. It is hard to imagine holiness or virtuosity of spirit apart from deeply felt compassion for those who suffer or from fierce anger at injustices worked against those who are vulnerable. Holy and virtuous people are not just those whose lives are directed by high principles of morality. They are the ones who are deeply moved by the experience of God's love and suffering touching human suffering and injustice within them. When this soulful desire to love begins to wane, we need to reawaken it through spiritual practices that open our interior space to the transforming power of God's Spirit. The way we are "moved" by our experience of God will influence our character and our actions. Spiritual renewal rekindles our longing for God and our desire to be our best selves in gracious response to God's loving us.

Imagination

The imagination, brain scientists tell us, is closely linked to mental, emotional, and sensory activities. It involves the whole person dealing with life as a whole.[29] So if you are suspicious of emotion as a source of truth, then you will be wary of the imagination as well. The problem with introducing the imagination is that we tend to think of it as the playground of artists, of people who make things up. If we equate the imagination with fiction, fantasy, and fairy tales, then we can easily ridicule or dismiss its significance. It seems to be the opposite of reason and objectivity. So bringing the imagination into a discussion of spirituality and morality would only seem to weaken the credibility of both. But far from endangering the spiritual and moral life, the imagination nurtures them.

By the imagination, I do not mean a gift some people have and others do not. It is not a capacity for frivolity in an otherwise serious world. As a resource to the spiritual and moral life, the imagination is not a flight of fancy. Nor is it a compartment of the personality along with the intellect and will. Rather, it is the very foundation for the activities of the intellect and will. By means of the imagination, we construct our world by bringing together diverse aspects of our experience into a meaningful whole.

One of the ways that the imagination connects the spiritual and moral life is through its interpretive function. As the way we make sense of things, the imagination is our prime means of perception.[30] We "see" by means of the imagination not just by taking a look, but even more by interpreting and valuing what we see. What we regard as worthy of our response depends on how we "see" it. For example, if I "see" that "my wife is a nag," "my employer is bossy," or "my students are eager," I will respond accordingly. In fact, most of our response is governed by what we see going on, not by conscious rational choice. For example, if we see our children as a burden, we refuse to carry them; if we look on our colleagues as competitors, we refuse to cooperate with them. These ways of seeing and acting have nothing to do with applying rules, but they have everything to do with responding to images. What we see sets the direction and limits of what we do; it generates certain options rather than others; and it disposes us to respond in one way rather than another. In the end, faith chooses the more adequate perspective from which to judge the event, but in the beginning it is the imagination that supplies the perspective. What is an option for someone else may never occur to us as one at all, for we simply don't see the world that way. We respond differently because we come from different places of emotion, imagination, and faith. We will change our moral behavior when we begin to experience life from a different point of view given to us by new images.

Since the interpretive function of the imagination is crucial for the moral life, the choice of images that we will allow to influence us is of primary importance. This is especially so because most of what we see does not lie in front of our eyes but behind them in the images that fill our imaginations. Roberto Benigni's Oscar-winning film, *Life Is Beautiful*, portrayed this power of the imagination quite effectively. In a world growing progressively darker by the advancing atrocities of Nazi occupation, Guido refuses to lose hope. He lives for his five-year-old son, Giosue, who is too young to understand the horrible evils of the Holocaust, but not too young to die. Guido resolves not to let the horror that surrounds them blind his son to the joys of being alive and being loved. Guido does this by reinterpreting the arrests, deportations, and harassments of the prison camps as all part of a continuous game. By re-imagining each potentially despairing incident as another phase of the game, Guido enables his son to remain largely unaware of the danger. Through his imagination shaped by his father, Giosue lives with hope in a universe of death.

We may want to criticize Guido for exploiting the power of the imagination to "make believe," because Guido's playful images do not ultimately awaken Giosue to the harsh reality of the prison camp. But, as the film shows so well, whether images are true or false, we live in the world of the images that we allow to dominate our imagination. Giosue could live with hope in a universe of death because his father cared for his soul by attending to his imagination with life-giving images. Giosue's loving attachment to his father enabled him to let his father's playful images have a greater influence on him than the images that were coming at him from the prison camp.

More than we may realize, our imagination is inherited from our social worlds. Our way of seeing is not so much as personal as it is a communal achievement. We do not come to any situation like blank film in a camera ready to record whatever is there. Our film has already been exposed to frameworks of meaning fashioned by the images we have inherited from our social worlds. Social scientists tell us that the images that fill our imaginations are largely the result of the beliefs and values, causes and loyalties of the communities that have the greatest influence on us. For example, Robert Bellah's sociological analysis underscores the influence that the American story of individualism has clearly had on us.[31] By living with this story, we have acquired a respect for autonomy as a value that we compromise only at our peril. This respect for autonomy is embedded in the Horatio Alger story and in the American dream. On the positive side, the right "to life, liberty, and the pursuit of happiness" has attracted the world's tired and poor. It also fuels the fires of ambition and creativity. On the negative side, it has led to the cruel treatment of Native Americans, to the exploitation of the environment, and to blaming the victims of poverty, injustice, and disease for their plight. The more we participate in the stories and language of the American Dream, the more we begin to take on its way of seeing and responding for better and for worse.

In other words, our imagination is almost totally dependent on the company we keep and the worlds we inhabit. For this reason, becoming morally mature and spiritually whole can never be merely an individual affair between "me and God." It can come only through social relationships. There's no other way. The full formation of a person involves participation in communities, in shared experiences, and through the example of others. After all, we acquire habits of the heart in the same way that we learn a language—by being immersed in its world so that we can observe and practice the behavior of others. Formation in virtue requires guiding images, or persuasive models of moral goodness.

In our time, the entertainment world is the "image industry" par excellence. Consider television, for example. News programs, soap operas, police dramas, cartoons, sporting events, situation comedies, and advertisements are the new gospel of our time. They have usurped the role of the church in shaping the imagination and our system of values.[32] Through visual and sound images, we begin to associate slick cars with power, sex with violence, social prestige with privilege, designer jeans with beautiful bodies. The images that come to us through the entertainment community with their message of the way life ought to be often stand in direct conflict with the images of the Gospels and rob religious stories and images of their power to move us. If we look on the world through the images of the media, we see that violence, consumerism, and exploitation characterize our life today. If our imaginations are filled with images of war, greed, corrupt power, competition, and exploitation, then we look on the world in a way that protects self-interest at the expense of everyone else. But if we look on the world through the images of covenant, creation, sin, incarnation, cross, and resurrection, for example, then we see a different world, where people need one another and work together for the well-being of all.

For good or ill, then, the communities that house the values to which we aspire shape us. That is why we need to be surrounded by allies, good friends, who think that living the moral life is worthwhile and that spirituality is truly a way of seeing, and then who live accordingly. We have to associate with people who are more morally mature and farther along the spiritual path than we are. We need mentors and models ("saints") to be our companions on the journey. The more we participate in the stories, rituals, language, and images of those who have a great influence on us, the more likely we are to be shaped by their values and way of seeing. We are socialized into morality and spirituality by the stories and images that have captured our imagination about how to understand ourselves and our experiences of life and death, success and failure, love and betrayal.

In addition to its interpretive function, the imagination also plays a creative function by helping us move into the future to create our world. So much of moral instruction is aimed at getting others to behave differently by trying to convert their wills. We try to reason with them, preach to them, badger them, or shame them into selflessness. But what is really at stake is not that they are stupid, selfish, closed, or uncaring. They simply lack imagination. They assume that what they are doing now is the only way to respond to the situation. They can't act differently because they can't imagine what it would be like to be someone else. If a possible way of acting is not perceived as being real, then we will never achieve it. Only if we can imagine a new way of life can we ever make it real for us. The bumper sticker that says "Imagine Peace" challenges us to imagine a world without war. If we can't, then we won't ever achieve it. There are many reasons that we might give to excuse ourselves from acting justly, but the primary one is that we can't imagine what it would look like to do so.

Christian spirituality and morality believe that the stories and images that come to us in the Christian story portray and describe goodness in the moral life, and they provide truthful ways of seeing the world. Undoubtedly, these stories and images will be in competition with others coming to us from the various worlds in which we live. Each world tries to tell us something about what is good and how life ought to be lived. The important question before us, then, is how decisive our Christian believing and beliefs ought to be for shaping our moral awareness. As James Gustafson would have it, "[they] ought to be the most decisive, most informing, most influencing beliefs and experiences in the lives of people."[33] However, how decisive they actually are will depend on how deeply one has appropriated them in becoming Christian. The incorporation of these stories into our way of seeing, feeling, thinking, judging, and acting will help us to engage the world as a people formed by Christian faith. Spiritual practices are very much part of the process by which we appropriate the images of the Christian story so that they shape our moral practices, our character and choices.

Body

Each person is uniquely constituted not only by spirit and soul (the noncorporeal dimensions) but also by the body. To be human before God is to be an embodied self. If spirit and soul are ways of looking at the self from the inside, the so-called interior life, the body is the way of looking at the self from the outside. The body is the self's opening to the world. It is the way souls meet. In and through our bodies we experience ourselves, others, the world, and God. In and through our bodies, we come to know and to love, to be known and to be loved by others. In the image of a ninth-century Irish teacher, John Scotus Eriugena, the body is "an echo of the soul." It reverberates the sounds from the depth of the self.[34]

The biblical view of the person appreciates the body as an integral expression of personal identity and not as something that belongs to the self as a possession. From such a view, to say, "That's my nose you are hitting" is no different from saying, "You're punching me." In short, "body" *(basar)* refers not to something one has but to one's self. The term *basar*, translated "flesh" or "body" but never as "corpse," can refer to an individual person or to the solidarity of persons in relationship, as the blood ties of kinship or the "two in one flesh" bond of husband and wife. To refer to the self from the perspective of *basar* is to emphasize the person as creature, absolutely dependent on God, weak and passing from this life. The body will return to dust (Gen 3:19; Job 34:15) while the spirit returns to God (Job 34:14; Eccl 12:7).[35] But never is *basar* used to distinguish a living physical being from a nonphysical spirit or soul. In the biblical view, spirit, soul, and body exist in mutual relationship. Human striving can lead to true self-realization only when these aspects of the self harmonize as a unified totality.[36]

The New Testament uses two words, *sarx* (flesh) and *soma* (body), to express *basar* of the Old Testament. Like *basar*, these two terms can refer to the tangible, biological part of the person as distinct from spirit and soul; they can also denote the individual person as a whole or the collective (e.g., Rom 6:12–13,19). However, the more typical Pauline practice is to contrast flesh and spirit. Flesh connotes the person left to oneself. To live according to the flesh leads to isolation and destruction. But to live by the spirit in our bodies is to be under God's influence and to attain personal integrity, happiness, and union with others (Gal 5:19–23).[37]

While "body" and "flesh" in Saint Paul can refer to human existence in its weakness subject to earthly tendencies, the "body" is also a holy source for living in the spirit glorifying God who came among us in the body of Jesus. The narrative of the incarnation provides the context for appreciating the fuller significance of this positive view of the body for spirituality and morality. Christian thinking about the body is based on the conviction of divine embodiment—God became human in Jesus. The mystery of the incarnation is a profound affirmation of the body. It proclaims that God comes to us in and through bodily form and that we, in turn, must relate to others, the world, and God in and through our bodiliness. It also helps us to appreciate embodiment in a way that is worthy of Paul's admonition, "glorify God in your body" (1 Cor 6: 20).

Yet this mystery of the incarnation, with its high valuation of things physical, has had a hard time securing a positive role for the body in spirituality and morality. The Christian tradition has been ambivalent about the body. On the one hand, the body is credited with being a good creation of God; on the other, ascetical practices soon developed a distrust of the body as an evil temptation to sin. The Gnostic and Manichean heresies, for example, with their view of the sinfulness of the flesh, have been officially repudiated, but they have not disappeared. Their devastating effects on Christian attitudes toward the body are still felt in the dualism that divides the material (body) from the spiritual (spirit and soul). This dualism has contributed to the misconception that authentic spirituality renounces the body, denies passions, and represses desires.

A major obstacle to a spirituality of the whole person is to see body, soul, and spirit as three uneasily aligned "components" rather than as forming an integrated reality—the embodied self. The integration of embodiment makes it impossible to draw a clear line marking where the inner world of spirit and soul ends and the world of the body begins. Just as the emotions share in rationality, so does the body. The body, too, is a way of knowing. Bodily reactions, and not just mental reasoning, affect our perception of what is going on and our evaluation of what is important.[38] The process of the discernment of spirits, for example, capitalizes on the wisdom of the body in the process of making a decision. If the body sends signals of distress when facing a certain behavior, then we may want to question or avoid that behavior. If the body sends signals of comfort, then we may be moving in the right direction.

Moreover, even apart from discernment, we have all met the truth of how perception and evaluation are characteristic of the entire embodied self, and not just of the brain, in our "Maalox moments." Remember how your body reacted when you did not feel up to the task you had to face, like a final exam, a job interview, or a new date? The body can't be fooled. Just the thought of facing these moments brought on bodily reactions—tense muscles, irritable bowel, sweating, weakness in the knees, a sudden loss of energy. Then, too, if you have ever tried to be creative when you had a sinus headache, you know how connected your body is to your inner spirit. Just as our bodily processes can be affected by our thoughts and attitudes, so our inner life can be nourished by bodily activities—dancing, swimming, hiking, receiving a massage, making love. Holistic medicine capitalizes on how our inner world has bodily repercussions and how taking care of our body can affect our inner world, and vice versa.

Such a holistic view of the person cannot tolerate a spirituality or morality that sees the body as somehow evil, belonging to a "lower nature," and needing to be conquered and controlled, while associating genuine spirituality and decent moral living with the mind and reason, the "higher nature." In a holistic view, the body is not something that must be tamed but claimed as an expression of one's self. In fact, some bodily form is our only way of presenting ourselves to others. The erotic, the sensuous, the emotional, and the passionate are not to be merely dismissed as threats to the spiritual and moral life, even if they must be focused to be useful. Spirituality and morality must be sensuous because we live in our bodies and express through them the deep desire of our spirit and the real feelings of our soul. So any attempt to relate spirituality and morality must take seriously the fact that the spirit does not float freely and that grace comes through the body. This truth lies at the heart of all incarnational theology.

Once we become convinced of our embodiment, then we can understand how attention to the needs of the body—good nutrition, rest, exercise, shelter, a supportive environment, and such—is not just part of our spiritual agenda but is a moral requirement as well. This attention to our own bodily life commits us to work for justice so that others may also have the necessities of bodily existence. If bodily life were an embarrassment to our spirituality, then we would lose our capacity for caring and for justice.

Moreover, as body-selves we are physical, sensuous, and sexual. As physical, we are never separate from the material world and so must live keenly aware of the limitations that come with having a body. We can't be everywhere at once nor do everything we would like. We have to prioritize our values and make trade-offs that respect our limits. Ascetical practices are ways of listening to our bodies, accepting limits, and living with balance. Furthermore, our connection to the material world and our sensuality can contribute to a stronger ecological consciousness and reverence for creation by making us aware of the Earth as a living organism to which we are interdependently connected.

As sensual and sexual we can be at home with pleasure and delight. Our sensuality is the way of incarnation. Remember, God deals with us through our senses. There's no other way for us who are body-persons. Our sensuality keeps us rooted in the physical world as the place of divine encounter. Our sexuality is embodied energy that gives us the capacity and desire to love and to bond with others. While the whole constellation of erotic energies, passion, and pleasure of bodily encounter are created goods, fragile and open to misuse, they ought not to be trivialized as too carnal to be spiritual. That was the mistake made by the Manichean heresy and other dualistic theologies. When the Song of Songs celebrates sexual pleasure and passion and when some of our classic mystics use sexual encounter to describe our ultimate union with God, they are on to something. They are reaching into the depths of that intimate relation between sexual and spiritual energies driving toward union. Sexuality enables us to find our full humanness not in isolation but in relationships, ultimately in relationship to God.[39]

Relationship is at the heart of our bodily existence. As embodied persons we are essentially relational, that is, open to the world, to others, and to God. So the way we express ourselves through our bodies becomes significant for the well-being of the community. The centrality of being in relationship for the spiritual and moral life is rooted in the uniquely Christian understanding of God as Trinity. Since we believe the Trinity to be a community of persons in loving relationship, we believe that to be made in the image of God is to be necessarily and inherently communal and relational. In this view, human relationships are a privileged locus for experiencing God, and authentic holiness is a communal affair. Chapter 4 will explore further implications of this image of God for the spiritual and moral life.

The communal, relational view of the self is a necessary corrective to the Enlightenment view of the person that has had a far-reaching influence on our spirituality and morality. The Enlightenment view of radical individualism thinks of the person as an individual first, not as a social being. As a result, it has focused our moral thinking too much on securing individual rights and liberties. The Enlightenment influence on our spirituality has made us too self-absorbed. Seeing the self as isolated, self-sufficient, and private, we thought we would better discover the true self by turning inward and disengaging from others. Solitude prevailed over community, and introspection became the primary tool of spiritual growth. Spirituality quickly became synonymous with self-help techniques and spiritual growth with self-improvement.

However, accepting the relational aspect of embodiment has refocused our attention on the fundamentally social character of being human. "We" comes before "I." Personal identity is a social identity. We know ourselves in relation to others. The "I" is a reflection of our knowing and loving and of how we have been known and loved. Once we accept ourselves as fundamentally social and existing in a web of interdependent relationships, then we know what it means to say, "We are in this together." Our individual life is always a life-with-others and personal flourishing is always entwined with the flourishing of others, including the Earth. There is no self-realization apart from responsibility for our neighbors and for the Earth. We discover ourselves not by retreating into solitude and disengaging from others but by being drawn into the lives of others. That is why we can say that, at bottom, morality and spirituality are a measure of the quality of our relationships.

The emphasis on the relational dimension of the embodied self has redirected spirituality from an overemphasis on the interior life to recognizing the centrality of being in right relationship with others. Michael Downey correctly notes that the turn to relationships for understanding the self naturally connects spirituality to the moral demands of creating a new social order based on mutuality, equality, and reciprocity rather than on domination and submission. Spiritual practices are no longer seen as aiming at self-purification and personal sanctification through self-denial but at establishing rightly ordered relationships with God, the wider human community, and the environment.[40] Since embodiment in its relational dimension makes a commitment to justice an integral aspect of spirituality, holiness necessarily includes an active concern for justice.[41]

Conclusion

Spirit, soul, and body are inseparably one. In fact, they are so intermingled that if we could somehow untangle them, we would cease to be human before God. But when we harmonize the rich constellation of meaning in each of these ways of seeing the person, then we come to the fuller reality to our humanness.[42] This exploration into an anthropology to undergird spirituality and morality reflects one of the insights of Karl Rahner's vision of the person as "spirit-in-the-world." That is, to be human is to be dynamically oriented toward God as the source, support, and goal of our restless desire to love and to be loved, to know and to be known, to be free and to set free.[43] This basic orientation to God constitutes the most radical meaning of what a human person is—a God-related being. We are not first constituted as human and then related to God. Our relationship to God makes us human. Because we are imprinted with the Spirit of God from the beginning, we are receiving Spirit and communicating it into all that we are and do. That is our spirituality. The public face of this communication is the moral life.

The good news of Christian faith is that God's loving us in the Spirit is the first principle on which we build a moral and spiritual life. As with any first principle, we cannot prove it but we can deduce from it. Once we accept it, then we can see how much follows from it. We can see that all life is lived in the presence of God, is a response to God, and has value in relation to God's love. This experience of being loved orients us toward a loving union or friendship with God where we show our love for

God by caring about what God cares about. In short, we are made out of love for love.

Caring about what God cares about is more than the sum of our reasons for acting. It involves affective, imaginative, and embodied aspects as well. We grasp values through our feelings, imagination, and body, and we in turn express what we value through them. The virtuous life, or being holy, is a life that expresses the divine love within us by engaging the whole self in caring about what God cares about. While reason draws insight from embodied experiences in order to understand what sort of personal and political life will be most fulfilling for humans, reason never acts without engaging the emotions, the imagination, and the body. The morality and spirituality of embodied human experience insist that bodily experiences reveal the divine, that the experience of the body's sensuality and sexuality is important in creating an ability to love others, and that the call to be loving is the call to become human in a social order where relations are ordered rightly with others, with the environment, and with God.

The quest to understand who we are as spiritual and moral persons is coupled with our desire to know God. So we must move from this search for being human before God to how it is that we experience God.

4.

Experiencing God

✵

The previous chapter focused on the human person as the subject of the experience of God. This chapter examines experiences of God and images of God and their influence on
spirituality and the moral life. Its conviction is that there can be
no morality or spirituality within the Christian framework that is
not grounded in God and in the experience of God in the Holy
Spirit. Thus, whether we experience God and how we experience God have a great deal to do with the content, tone, and
quality of our spirituality and moral life.

Where Is Your God?

What would you do if you were ever confronted directly with a
sign of God's presence? Agnostic Anne Edwards, a leading character in Mary Doria Russell's religious/science fiction novel *The
Sparrow*, ponders this question in her search for a confident
sense that God is really present in the universe, making sense of
things. She knew that in the Bible, when people confronted God

at Sinai and again in Jerusalem at the cross, they turned back to their common life. She muses:

> Faced with the Divine, people took refuge in the banal, as though answering a cosmic multiple-choice question: If you saw a burning bush, would you (a) call 911, (b) get the hot dogs, or (c) recognize God? A vanishingly small number of people would recognize God, Anne had decided years before, and most of them had simply missed a dose of Thorazine.[1]

Where can you point in your life and say that God is there? Have you ever had an experience of God? These are hard questions to answer when asked so directly. They seem like we are being asked to lasso the wind. What makes them hard is the peculiar nature of the experience of God. It is obscure and often goes unnoticed because God is not a direct object of experience the way a tree is, for example, which imposes itself on our senses so that we immediately recognize it. The experience of God is not one more experience that we can place alongside of or in addition to other experiences of nature, people, or events. Rather, the experience of God is a special dimension of every experience, and we speak of experiencing God indirectly through the experience of something else.

So let's take another tack on retrieving an experience of God. Recall times when you were surprised, especially those times when you experienced more than you expected. Often, these are the kinds of experiences that practically take our breath away. (Remember, "spirituality" is rooted in the Hebrew word *ruah* or "breath," usually translated as "spirit.") Sometimes these experiences evoke from us the spontaneous exclamation, "Oh, my God!"

In Oscar Hijuelos's novel, *Mr. Ives' Christmas*, Edward Ives has an experience of God while standing on the corner of Madison and Forty-First Street in downtown Manhattan. As the story goes, he steps out of his office building into the crisp clear air of the Christmas season. While standing at the corner waiting for the light to change, and in an unforgettable moment of pure clarity, he "began to feel *euphoric*, all the world's goodness, as it were, spinning around him."[2] He was overwhelmed with joy and felt connected to all things. The people all around him truly seemed blessed. Then, catching his own reflection in a window, Ives "judged himself a most pleasant-looking, perhaps saintly, fellow."[3] He explains his joy and renewed appreciation of himself and all that surrounded him as an experience of God's Spirit in the world.

For Mr. Ives, an experience of God happened in downtown Manhattan. Someone else might speak of their experience of God by recalling how they were ambushed by awe when driving along the highway, rounding a bend, and coming upon a breathtaking vista of a valley nestled between sharply rising snow-covered mountains. They are fascinated, struck with awe: "My God, isn't this beautiful!" Others remember a terrifying sight of horrible violence. It may have been a TV news clip or a neighborhood drive-by shooting. It makes them tremble. They are left breathless: "My God, isn't this horrible!" These vastly contrasting experiences can be moments of epiphany for the believer. They are intuitional insights into the deeper dimensions of the moment.

THE CALL TO HOLINESS

The surprise or shock element tugs at our awareness that there is a deeper mystery to life than what meets the eye. This deeper mystery is God reaching out to us, calling us into relationship (through our spirituality) and to a response (through our moral life). In one instance, it can be our interdependence with all things and our responsibility to care for one another and the Earth. In another, it can be our solidarity with all peoples and our responsibility to protect human life. In each instance, we feel drawn out of ourselves and into deeper communion with nature or with humanity; and, in being so drawn, we feel called to be responsible for more than ourselves. In those human moments there is divine communication awaiting a response. How we respond shapes and is shaped by our moral character.

One lesson this approach teaches us is that our experience does not disclose the Spirit of God for us if we remain detached observers. We must be involved in the experience and feel it from the inside. We become aware of the presence of God in the Holy Spirit through a felt perception. This means we experience God in the Spirit when we are "struck by" or "moved by" a mysterious dimension of experience that is greater than what meets the eye. God may be present in our world, but that does not mean that we always see God there. Remember, the spiritual life is, at root, a matter of seeing, of seeing God in more and more places of our life and linking all that makes up our life to God. Only in faith can we see everything as linked to God as the source of our lives, animating, empowering, and renewing us, and as the object of our longing for love, for meaning, and for purpose. In the end, we name the experience as an experience of God in the Spirit or not because it rings true or not with what we know of the nature of God. So how we are taught about God and treated in the name of God are important for recognizing the divine presence in our experiences.

The "In and Through" Approach to God

In the Judeo-Christian tradition, the God who is with us (immanence) is also the God who is totally other (transcendence). When we accept the total otherness of God, we admit that we cannot experience God immediately, but only in a mediated way. There is no other way for us who are body-persons. Without our bodily senses and the imagination, God's word to us could not get through. We do not "leap-frog" creation to reach the Creator. God's way to us and our way to God is in and through the human, the fleshy, the historical, the particular. There is no other way for us who are body-persons to experience the invisible except through that which invades the senses.

Our experience of God in the Spirit cannot be dissociated from our experience of the world around us. One of the most ancient Christian perceptions is that there are traces of the divine in all of creation. There is not one world of action, places, people, or events that are remote from and untouched by grace and another world that is sacred, where God dwells. The whole universe is the dwelling place of God. All things are sacred and natural at the same time. We live in a sacramental universe.

A human story that illustrates this so well is the story of Helen Keller. Helen's world was a world of particulars, sensations of odor, taste, and touch. There was no light or sound. At first the movements of her teacher's hand in her own did not disclose anything beyond tactile pressure. Then one day a whole new world opened up for Helen. She learned that a touch could point beyond itself to something more. That day Helen realized a deeper dimension of reality that was there all the time, but she had never "seen" it. Here is Helen's account of that eventful day:

> We walked down the path to the well-house, attracted by the fragrance of the honeysuckle with which it was covered. Someone was drawing water and my teacher placed my hand under the spout. As the cool stream gushed over one hand she spelled into the other the word *water*, first slowly, then rapidly. I stood still, my whole attention fixed upon the motions of her fingers. Suddenly I felt a misty consciousness as of something forgotten—a thrill of returning thought; and somehow the mystery of language was revealed to me. I then knew that "w-a-t-e-r" meant the wonderful cool something that was flowing over my hand. That living word awakened my soul, gave it light, hope, joy, set it free!...As we returned to the house every object which I touched seemed to quiver with life. That was because I saw everything with the strange, new sight that had come to me.[4]

Helen's experience is a living example of the incarnational principle—the human, the fleshy, the concrete can point to an invisible reality. Incarnational faith is like the way Helen "saw" water. This faith opens our eyes to see that we no longer stop at the appearance of things, but see through them to the deeper reality in which we live. For persons of faith, the world of experience speaks of God's presence. This means that any event of history or wonder of creation can mediate God's presence in the Spirit. The pre-eminent mediation, or incarnation, of God for us is Jesus Christ.

The incarnational principle says that our experience of God comes *in and through* something else. Everything that exists is rooted in the gracious self-communication of God in the Spirit. Every element of creation is haunted by a presence beyond itself. That is, it is potentially a medium of God's self-gift. Thus, to grasp anything in its depth is to discover grace, to experience God's presence in the Holy Spirit. When we no longer have eyes to see that the stuff of our daily life points beyond itself, then the spiritual life withers and, with it, morality.

The Bible knows this "in and through" approach to God well. It does not know any substantive distinction between the action of God and historical events. Everything is at one and the same time caused by God and by natural forces within the world. No wonder, then, that nature, historical events, and people (preeminently Jesus) are the primary media in and through which the Bible speaks of experiencing God.

The Exodus from Egypt, that formative experience of Israel becoming the People of God, can serve as a good example of how this approach works in the Bible. First comes the experience. Moses leads a band of slaves to freedom. After the liberation comes the sharing of the experience by telling the story over again. Through storytelling, a growing awareness dawns that recognizes not Moses but God as the one who freed the slaves and made them a people. Then annual celebrations of the event continue to make the presence and action of God in this liberating event alive for each generation. Retelling the story of Exodus as one's own story evokes new experiences of a liberating God that shed light on the present and opened the future to a fresh response to God through liberating deeds. The God who once freed slaves held in bondage continues to call the people of every age who live by this story to a freedom they may only dimly perceive.

The Exodus establishes the recurring biblical story line: God frees people from a death-dealing situation for a new life that they are free to choose and pursue. The Christian people see in and through the life, death, and glorification of Jesus not only the continuation of this story, but also the revelation of new depths of God's loving, sustaining graciousness that gives us the assurance of final victory. The story of Jesus assures us that life is stronger than death, and that grace abounds greater than sin. This is the story we live by.

The pattern of this story is also the movement from spirituality to the moral life. Notice the pattern. First, experience. Everyday experience is the entryway into the spiritual dimension of our life. Then comes awareness that there is something more to the experience than meets the eye. From this spiritual awakening comes recognition: "Oh, my God!" "God is touching me!" "I have seen the Lord!" From recognizing God at work in our lives comes celebration, prayers of praise and thanksgiving: God is here! Let's celebrate! Praise the Lord! From celebration comes our moral response: Because we have been liberated, out of praise and thanksgiving we must do liberating deeds!

The theology of the "in and through" approach tells us that every human experience, if given a chance, can speak to us of God. Mystics and poets know this. Pierre Teilhard de Chardin's "divine milieu," Elizabeth Barrett Browning's "earth's crammed with heaven," and Gerard Manley Hopkins's "the world is charged with the grandeur of God," say it in other words. The spiritual director's question, "Where do you find God in this?" is grounded in this "in and through" approach to God. It is rooted in the conviction that God comes to us in and through our everyday experiences where God is calling us to life, growth, and wholeness.

The "in and through" approach begins with the presupposition that the world as graced is haunted by the Holy Spirit. We cannot induce God's presence, conjure it, or create it. God's coming is always God's own graciously free and loving action. It is gift. Our task is not to make God present, as though God were missing. God is already always and everywhere present to us, but we have to desire to be present and receptive to God. We cannot do God's part. All we can do is the human part as well as we can. Our part is to be open, to receive, to embrace, and then to respond. It is just as the Sufi Master claims: Once upon a time, a seeker ran through the streets shouting over and over again, "We must put God in our lives." "Ah," smiled the Master, "if only we realized that God is always already in our lives. Our spiritual task is to recognize this." This is spirituality and morality in practice.

To say that God is already present to us means that we are never out of touch with God, even though we may not be attending to the presence of God. To experience God is to be aware that we are related to a larger mystery within which we live. Saint Paul understood this well when he expressed the following in his speech in the Areopagus at Athens: "Indeed he is not far from each one of us. For 'in him we live and move and have our being'" (Acts 17:27–28). For this reason, our relationship to God and response to God cannot be restricted to special activities or special moments. God is not out there beyond the realm of our everyday life. All experiences are at least an implicit experience of God, for we live in the presence of an ever-present God. Spiritual growth is becoming more aware of this mystery that is at the heart of every moment.

Yet, for so many, God seems hard to find. It is hard to focus on the transcendent when the tug of the immanent is so strong. Before they can experience God, some people must overcome obstacles that seem insurmountable. Mary Doria Russell's *The Sparrow* can be read as an extended parable of the risks of religious faith in the face of evil. One of its major characters, Emilio Sandoz, is a Jesuit priest whose faith is the model for any believer who must face setbacks, betrayal, or evil of any sort. When confronted with the absence of God, he defends God as the one who watches over, rejoices over, and weeps with humankind. But he is challenged by Matthew 10:29: "Are not two sparrows sold for a penny? Yet not one of them will fall to the ground apart from your Father." How can we believe in God's loving presence and care for us if the sparrow still falls under God's watchful eye?[5]

The fallen sparrow and other obstacles to faith are variations of the unanswerable question of evil. Why, if God cares for us, do we have AIDS, the holocaust, famine, war, and other evils? In such senseless, tragic, and cruel events, the spiritual director's question, "Where is God in all this?" only seems to echo in a hallow cavern. These events are indeed insurmountable for those who do not believe that God is present there, too. For the believer, God is found in and through the one with AIDS, and in and through the one who serves with love and tenderness. We find God in and through one another. God is grieving with us in our pain, working with us to bring good from evil, and calling us to change the conditions that make people suffer. We know God's love, compassion, and mercy in and through the love, compassion, and mercy that we receive and share. At least that is the way it was for one woman who sat in prayerful anguish with an eleven-year-old girl racked with uncontrollable pain from a spinal problem. In her prayer, she felt God's presence this way: "It is I who am in an agony in this young girl and it is I who scream through her, and it is I too who am in a compassionate agony in you on her behalf."[6] The Taize chant puts this insight into music using the ancient Latin refrain *"Ubi caritas et amor, Deus ibi est."* This is the same message that Saint John reminds us: "God is love, and those who abide in love abide in God, and God abides in them" (1 John 4:16).

Putting the accent on the ordinary as the place of experiencing God in the Spirit keeps us attentive to what is going on inside us and around us. Spiritual practices are ways to nurture that attentiveness. Take contemplative prayer, for example. It is the discipline of sharpening our vision to see God at work drawing all things to their fulfillment, and it is noticing all that prevents this fulfillment from happening. This kind of prayer is more than rote and ritual. It is a deeper seeing into things and a resulting reverence. The deeper seeing is a grasp of the public, social significance of our experiences of God. The resulting reverence is our moral response that is our spirituality in practice. Notice the pattern: Loving attention to God as the source of all things (our spirituality) stirs a reverent response for all things in relation to God (our moral life).

Out of such reverence we partner with God's work of enabling all things to come to their fulfillment. We do this when we let go of control and suppress our suspicions; when we forgive and seek reconciliation; when we raise children who aspire to a higher goal than looking out for themselves; when we work together to preserve the environment and stop seeing the world as a resource to use rather than a life-support system to protect; when we work to put an end to violence, hunger, homelessness, and disease; when we treat others with the dignity they deserve as images of God; it happens, in short, when we listen closely to the yearnings of the human heart, have our breath taken away, and allow ourselves to be struck by awe, wonder, and surprise. When we are struck by "Oh, my God, this is beautiful," we work to preserve it; and, when we are left breathless by "Oh, my God, this is horrible," we try to change it. This is our prayer nurturing reverence and giving rise to moral action. Our experience of God gives rise to our response to God by cooperating with the action of God's Spirit at work transforming the world.

The Depth Dimension of All Experience

Experiences of God in the Spirit often elude us because we are looking in the wrong place, or our "God glasses" are so distorted that our vision is blurred. A commonly held notion about experiencing God is that one's relationship with God is realized only in explicitly religious activities. But contemporary theology is helping us respect the richness of the mystery of God by focusing our vision on the depth dimension of all experience. Grace in human life is not a special zone outside of which is the purely secular and profane. Rather than putting God in a box and thinking of distinct realms where we might experience God (such as church, sacraments, prayer), contemporary theology points to the deepest dimension of all experience. It has made us aware that there is far more to life than we have settled for.

John Shea shows how one boy found God with this simple story of a family tradition of sharing a group grace before a festive holiday meal. We pick up on the story when the turn comes to the youngest, a five-year-old boy. Shea continues,

> He began by thanking the turkey which, although he had not yet tasted it, he was sure it would be good. This was a novel piece of gratitude and he followed it with more predictable credits given to his mother for cooking the turkey and his father for buying it. Then he began a chain of thank-yous, surfacing hidden benefactors and linking them together. "And the checker at the Jewel, and all the Jewel people, and the farmers who feed the turkeys to get them fat, and the people who make the feed, and the people who bring the

119

turkeys to the store...." His little Colombo mind was playing detective, tracing the path of the turkey to his plate. This litany went on for some time and ended with, "Did I miss anyone?"

"God," said his older brother.

"I was just getting to him," the child solemnly said, unflustered.[7]

Shea uses this story to show how this budding theologian gets to God through human experience. Other contemporary theologians agree.

Paul Tillich, one of the great American Protestant theologians of the past century, puts it this way:

The name of this infinite and inexhaustible depth and ground of all being is God. That depth is what the word God means. And if that word has not much meaning for you, translate it, and speak of the depths of your life, of the source of your being, of your ultimate concern, of what you take seriously without any reservation.[8]

As long as we skim the surface of life, running from one thing to another, we miss the mystery of God. But when we slow down and "take time to smell the roses," as the saying goes, and touch the depth of the beauty of nature, the passion of love, or the agony of loss, for example, then we find God. Tillich turns our gaze from looking up in search of God to looking deeply within. When we are more attuned to the depths of all that is around us, the depth of our relationships, or the depths of our own self, then we are more aware of God.

For Karl Rahner, perhaps the greatest Catholic theologian of the twentieth century, the experience of God constitutes "the ultimate depths and the radical essence of *every* spiritual and personal experience (of love, faithfulness, hope, and so on)."[9] While all experiences of life provide the locus for our experience of God in the Spirit, certain experiences manifest this depth dimension more clearly than others. These "signals of transcendence" are experiences that underscore the mystical depths of the person. Rahner acknowledges that we readily associate positive experiences with this sacramental function, such as experiences of natural beauty that fill us with awe or experiences of human love that make us feel worthy and blessed. These kinds of experiences support our attitude of trust toward life and fill us with gratitude. But Rahner also recognizes that the not so pleasant experiences in life can also be experiences of the Spirit. He offers a set of questions that point to the transcendent at the depths of our lives:

> Have we ever kept silent, despite the urge to defend ourselves, when we were being unfairly treated? Have we ever forgiven another although we gained nothing by it and our forgiveness was accepted as quite natural? Have we ever made a sacrifice without receiving any thanks or acknowledgment, without even feeling any inward satisfaction? Have we ever decided to do a thing simply for the sake of conscience, knowing that we must bear sole responsibility for our decision without

being able to explain it to anyone? Have we ever tried to act purely for love of God when no warmth sustained us, when our act seemed a leap in the dark, simply nonsensical? Were we ever good to someone without expecting a trace of gratitude and without the comfortable feeling of having been "unselfish"?[10]

Other experiences, both positive and negative, can be added where we have a felt sense that there is more to the moment than what we can account for. In Mark Salzman's novel, *Lying Awake*,[11] epileptic seizures are the medium of divine disclosure for Sister John of the Cross, the main character. In her book, *This Blessed Mess*, Patricia Livingston reflects on convictions that sustain her when life gets chaotic and seems to be falling apart. She trusts in the revelation of 1 John 4:16 and feels the presence of God in experiences of love.[12] In his book, *Creative Spirituality*, Robert Wuthnow reviews the "moments of transcendence" reported by artists to show that the creative process offers an awareness that something beyond the ordinary exists. For example, Katie Agresta, a composer of music, says, "I almost feel like somebody else wrote it." Poet Greg Glazner says, "It's just a sense of being connected to something a lot bigger than you are, so that it's no longer about your own ego." A painter says, "There are some times when I don't know where that energy is coming from. The brush leads me and it seems to have nothing to do with my body. It is coming purely from the spirit."[13]

Others who have shared their experiences of God with me have told stories of both positive and negative experiences, like living out of the depth of their conviction without regard for public approval or personal consequence; they have spoken of a deep loneliness, of emptiness and an immense longing that could not be filled by making one more dollar, or meeting one more person, or getting one more promotion; they have also spoken of facing serious illness and the threat of death as well as experiences of peaceful deaths of loved ones; they have spoken of the birth of their children, of sitting with their grandfather along the river bank fishing, of solitary walks along the shore and of quiet listening to music; they have spoken of personal acts of creativity; and they have spoken of the joys of sex, of friendship, and of being surprised by the loving kindness that goes beyond what we owe one another. All of these experiences can be moments of grace, but since they do not impose themselves on us as an undeniable fact of God's Spirit touching us, they can be easily ignored or explained away. However, in the Rahnerian spirit, we who live by faith have in fact experienced God as something more than and different from a part of our world. Epiphanies are everywhere for those whose "God glasses" are in focus.

Some people see things more clearly than the rest of us. Artists and poets seem to do it best. They help us see and experience the world more transparently than we might without them. Our religious poets, the psalmists, for example, were adept at finding God everywhere. For example, Psalm 19 opens with this awareness: "The heavens are telling the glory of God; and the firmament proclaims his handiwork" (v. 1). Psalm 104 continues in awe: "O Lord, how manifold are your works! In wisdom you have made them all" (v. 24). Psalm 139 expresses the ever-present reality of a gracious God:

Where can I go from your spirit?
   Or where can I flee from your presence?
If I ascend to heaven, you are there;
   if I make my bed in Sheol, you are there.
If I take the wings of the morning
   and settle at the farthest limits of the sea,
even there your hand shall lead me,
   and your right hand shall hold me fast. (vv. 7–10)

Jesus, too, was adept at finding God in the ordinary. The fundamental message of Jesus about God is that human life is the home of God. We need not look anywhere else. All the parables of Jesus are stories about experiencing God in ordinary life. His stories are filled with very human characters and very human experiences—seeds, a change of seasons, the action of yeast in dough, guests at a banquet, a woman cleaning her house, bride and groom, parents and children, rich people and beggars. While none of the parables ever mentions "God" directly, they all express a contemplative vision and express the conviction that God comes to us through daily events and, often, from quite unexpected sources and people. The great reversals in the parables attest to God as the God of the unexpected. The message of the parables is clear: Pay attention! They tell us over and over again that if we want to know where to look for God, then watch for the surprises! In the fabric of ordinary life, something extraordinary is happening. In the unexpected surprises the discerning believer sees another dimension, the Spirit of God. So, to experience God we do not need to look up to heaven but across to one another and within our own hearts, for the ordinary resonates with the extraordinary, at least for those who have eyes to see and ears to hear.

What the Bible, Tillich, and Rahner seem to be telling us, then, and what so many people searching for God force us to admit, is that if it makes sense to speak of God at all, then we must be able to experience God in the Spirit where we spend most of our time and expend most of our energy. Every human experience, if given a chance, can point beyond itself to something more. We must cease trying to confine the experience of God's Spirit to specifically religious sectors of life. If we were to so confine God, then we would be forced to turn away from the ordinary experiences of life in order to be touched by the gracious reality of God. But the Bible and these theologians are telling us that the entire world is enchanted, filled with God's Spirit.

Yet people miss experiencing the Spirit of God in more and more places in their lives because their "God glasses" are out of focus. Anne Lamott provides a good example of the need for corrective lenses:

> I was remembering an old story the other day about a man getting drunk at a bar in Alaska. He's telling the bartender how he recently lost whatever faith he'd had after his twin-engine plane crashed in the tundra.
>
> "Yeah," he says bitterly. "I lay there in the wreckage, hour after hour, nearly frozen to death, crying out for God to save me, praying for help with every ounce of my being, but he didn't raise a finger to help. So I'm done with that whole charade."

"But," said the bartender, squinting with an eye at him, "you're here. You *were* saved."

"Yeah, that's right," says the man. "Because finally some goddamn *Eskimo* came along...."[14]

This man at the bar does not yet know the God who acts in all human experience in ways that satisfy our deepest longing for life and liberty, for healing and wholeness, for solidarity and justice, for joy and peace. To find God we don't have to look up from the people and events in life but more deeply into them. But, as the saying goes, "We walk through mysteries as a child scuffles through daisies." When everydayness ceases to be a vessel of mystery, then we have lost our occasion for encountering the Holy. Epiphanies are everywhere for those who are willing to search for them in what might seem to be the strangest of places.

Who Is Your God?

Talk of experiencing God's Spirit presumes that we know the kind of God we are experiencing. After all, don't we all believe in the same God? Obviously not. There may be superficial agreement on the word but not on the image. A morality that rises out of spirituality is informed by the kind of God we experience and is concerned to know what difference it makes. Our images of God not only say something about who God is for us, but also have moral implications. That is, they say something about who we are now, who we ought to become, and what we ought to do in relation to God and to all that God cares about. Images of God evoke corresponding affections that dispose us to act in certain ways. Because the images of God that fill our imagination influence the way we understand God, ourselves, and the way we respond to the world around us, they are very important for relating spirituality to morality.

In chapter 2, we saw that the legal model of morality reigned for a long time. During its reign, we burned a lot of incense at the shrine of an all-time favorite God — the God of law and order. This God goes by the alias "The Boss Man Upstairs," or "Resident Policeman." This is the "gotcha" God who is on the prowl, keeps book on us, waits for us to trip up so that we can be marked a loser, and threatens to imprison us if we get out of line. An image of God like this nurtures fear as the motivating force in the moral life. It leads to a preoccupation with sin, with just how far we can go, and with a scrupulosity about how much we need to do to fulfill our obligations. Rewards are expected for those who fulfill God's commands and punishment for those who do not. Such an image of God evokes a spirituality that is passive and a moral life that is timid.

The images we have of God, like the one of an ultra-demanding, punitive God, are functions of our religious imagination. The imagination, remember, is not a flight into fantasy. It is an important spiritual and moral capacity for making sense out of our world. The importance of images and the imagination in spirituality and morality cannot be overstated.[15] Through images in the imagination, we organize and interpret what is going on around us so that we can make sense of the diverse experiences of our life. Images are not to be equated with visual fantasy or the Disney world of make-believe. Rather, images are structures of human knowing. They focus a whole complex of conscious and unconscious ideas, feelings, perspectives, and associated experiences. Our images of God are the most influential images for our spirituality and morality because our whole worldview is interested in them, and they control how we relate to God.

Most of us have picked up our images of God from religious stories we have heard, artwork we have seen, and the way we have been taught about God, especially through the way we have been treated in the name of God and according to God's will. Our images of God are hard to shake. Even as adults, we still burn incense at the shrine of the law-and-order God. Images seem to have embedded themselves in the elusive corners of our subconscious and continue to influence our convictions and experiences of God and of ourselves. They affect our feeling for what it is like to live in relationship to God, and they especially affect the attitude we bring to our spiritual practices, where we attend to the presence of God, and to our moral lives, where we express our response to God.

Just as we tried to retrieve an experience of God at the beginning of this chapter, I invite you to identify the image of God that is most powerful for you. How would you describe it? If you had to paint it, what would it look like? When Edward Ives's son Robert asked him what God looked like, Ives told him, "God is spirit," and he imagined God "as a vaporous goodness inside people's being."[16] God's most common form for Mr. Ives was "the goodness and piety of others."[17] Some who have shared their images of God with me have used a flame, a rose, the sun,

the ocean, a chariot driver, a cathedral, the Pietà, a human figure with a ball and chain attached at the ankle, a womb.

Images as Metaphors

Images give us access to God, but images are always limited
expressions of God. So a word of caution is in order before going
too far into exploring images of God. Images are dangerous
because we can take them literally and make any single image
absolute. Instead of giving rise to reflection and response, they
can paralyze the heart and the mind into a limited concept of
God. Images of God are simultaneously true and untrue. The
whole array of images limits and qualifies one another. No image
is an adequate picture of God, because all of our knowledge of
God and ways of talking about God are analogical. That is to say,
there is some likeness and unlikeness of God in the medium we
use to express God. When it comes to God, metaphors limp; no,
they scarcely crawl. But metaphors are all we have. They may
not be what God is, but they are better than nothing at all. Since
we believe that God has become human in Jesus, we believe that
we can find traces of the mystery of God's Spirit within human
experiences. Although human metaphors are more unlike than
they are like some aspect of God, we accept the limits of language and experience so that we can appreciate the dim light the
metaphor sheds on the mystery that is beyond all imagining.

The incomprehensible mystery of God makes it appropriate to speak of God in nonpersonal terms such as Tillich's
"ground of being" or Rahner's "holy mystery." But it is also
appropriate to speak of God in personal terms to express God's

relationship to the world. In either case, we must speak of God in human language. It's all we have. Yet God is always more than what our language can express. It is possible that some people have lost faith today because they have taken literal interpretations of limited images of God (such as God is father; God is masculine) for the whole reality of God. Their quarrel is with the image, not with the actual mystery of God. That is why the divine command against making idols and worshiping them (Exod 20:4–5) applies as much to images of the imagination as it does to statues and paintings. The revelation of the divine name to Moses at the burning bush (Exod 3:13–15) reminds us that God is unnamable. So we must rotate our images of God through our awareness and prayer lest we deceive ourselves into believing that any single image of God is the incomprehensible reality of God. The full significance of any one image can be seen only in relation to a wealth of divine images. It is the wide range of images that reminds us that God cannot be restricted to any single image but transcends them all.

The Bible witnesses to a many-sided God by using a great variety of images: father, mother, lover, husband, king, judge, creator, eagle, lion, potter, rock, fortress, whirlwind, to name a few. In the "in and through" approach to God, the imagery we use for God emerges from the medium through which we encounter God. For example, if nature is our primary medium, we may prefer images of God as creator, rock, or whirlwind. If an historical event is our medium, we may prefer images of deliverer, fortress, or refuge. If people are the media for encountering God, we may use father, mother, lover, friend, and so forth.

In the "in and through" approach to God, images say something about the inherent quality of God and something about our experience of and ongoing relationship to God. To say God is "lover," for example, is to say something about the inherent quality of God as love and also something about our experience of being loved and our relationship to God as continuing to love us. The "in and through" approach is what keeps the reality of God joined to the reality of the human experiences in and through which we encounter God. This is what allows us to say that in and through our love for one another we become aware of a greater Love sustaining us. In and through our experience of accepting and being accepted, we become aware of a greater Acceptance receiving us. While we may take our images of God from the medium of encounter, we live with an image because it rings true to our experience.

Images of God and Morality

The theological tradition also witnesses to many facets of God through the images it has used to express the incomprehensible mystery of God. The experience of God mediated through these images engenders certain sorts of awareness and qualities of character that shape our spirituality and moral life. Without pretending to be exhaustive, James Gustafson in his book *Can Ethics Be Christian?*[18] draws out some of the moral implications of certain images of God. Three of his examples will suffice here.

The image of God as Creator expresses the experience of living in reliance upon others, upon culture, and upon nature. These experiences open us to an ultimate dependence on the source of all being, God the Creator. The sense of dependence entails the moral responsibility to be stewards of creation who seek to preserve the good that God has created. It also engenders the virtue of humility, whereby we live with the limitations of created reality, have a critical sense about ourselves and what we produce, and foster interdependence with one another and with all creation. The sense of dependence also engenders the disposition to trust in God as ultimately sustaining us. This trust releases the freedom to risk something new and to act under conditions of less than complete certainty with the confidence that God continues to provide new possibilities for sustaining the well-being of creation.

The image of a beneficent God reflects the experience of being loved freely. This experience of being so loved calls forth the virtue of gratitude. At the heart of a morality grounded in the experience of a beneficent God is the response of seeking the good of others in gratitude for the goodness bestowed on us. What we have received freely, we ought to give freely. When we experience God's giving graciously, we infer that we ought to care for what has been given to us and share it freely, graciously, and lovingly.

The third image, God as end, engenders confidence that life has meaning, value, and purpose, even though we may not see the meaning or purpose at the moment. A restless longing animates spirituality and the moral life. At some level we are always dissatisfied with everything. Nothing we have been able to find satisfies us. This feeling of being always dissatisfied at the deepest level points to God as our end. To be fundamentally directed toward God as our end gives a sense of coherence to the fragments and brokenness we find in life. This image of God gives us a sense of direction, too. We seek to care about what God cares about by realizing those values that are in accord with what God values—the well-being of all.

These are but three examples of spiritual and moral dimensions implied in three classical images of God. Another classic image that has wide-ranging implications for spirituality and morality is God as Trinity, an image that elaborates the central belief about God in the Christian faith—that God is love. It expresses the experience of God's free and total self-giving love. Unfortunately the doctrine of the Trinity has been neglected for too long in the spiritual and moral life. To the extent that we think of the Trinity as an old man, a boy, and a bird, or treat the Trinity as an insoluble arithmetic problem (How can $3 = 1$?), then we miss the central theme of all trinitarian theology: God's nature is relational, a community of persons radically equal to each other and bonded in a mutual outpouring of love. Since we are created in this divine likeness, we can infer that we are social by nature and made to share. Our best analogy for understanding the Trinity is that of the dance. (In fact, the Greek word *perichoresis*, used to describe how the three persons in the Trinity relate, is the source of our word *choreograph*—to design a dance). Our God as Trinity is the dance of love, a mutual giving and receiving of love. The very nature of God is to overflow with an overwhelming gift of love for which our only response can be gratitude. As Catherine LaCugna's research on the Trinity has helped us to appreciate, God is no self-contained entity far removed from us. God is a dynamic personal relationship of love both with us and for us.[19]

The image of God as Trinity implies something important about ourselves, too. As Michael and Kenneth Himes have shown, the trinitarian doctrine implies a communitarian understanding of being human.[20] In fact, our capacity for relationships ultimately binds us to God. We are persons by virtue of relationship to one another, and sustaining a loving relationship with all things is the good we long for. The trinitarian vision sees that no one exists by oneself, but only in relationship to others. To be is to be in relationship. The individual and community co-exist. Just as God is loving communion of persons in relationship, so we who are images of God are to discover ourselves in relationships. To think of a person without thinking of that person in relationship to another is to miss what it means to be a person. From this understanding of being person we can derive a fundamental human right—the right to participate in the life of the human community. Humanness and relationality are proportional to one another. The more deeply we participate in relationships, the more human we become.

The moral implication of this trinitarian foundation for personhood is that we realize our humanness to the extent that we choose to be related, that is, to love. We do this when we attend to the worth and dignity of others. This can be expressed as simply as by paying attention to the cashier at the grocery store or as elaborately as by making a public apology seeking forgiveness from those we have offended by mistreatment. The freedom that we need for living morally is the freedom to give of ourselves more completely. A deeper participation in the human community enhances the humanity of each person, while the failure to establish community diminishes the humanity of all. The doctrine of the Trinity calls us to create a community of sisters and brothers characterized by equality, mutuality, and reciprocal giving and receiving for the sake of the well-being of each person, the whole community, and the whole Earth. This doctrine also calls us to challenge any structures or relations that subordinate, marginalize, or exclude. An interpersonal relationship of love and justice is both the norm against which to measure relationships among persons and between human beings and the Earth and the goal toward which we ought to strive in our relationships.

In a trinitarian spirituality, we do not need to inject God from the outside because God is already present as the inner dynamic of community drawing us together. This spiritual vision is captured very effectively in the famous icon of the Trinity painted by Andrei Rublev. The icon depicts the three persons of God sitting at a table and pointing to the chalice, the symbol of God's overflowing love. It is so painted as to make a place at the table for the viewer. The viewer feels invited to sit at the table with the three persons to share in the divine community. Viewing this icon gives us a glimpse of God's desire for us to be drawn into union with the community of life that is God.

A student shared a similar experience of feeling part of a living icon while attending Sunday liturgy at Holy Spirit Parish/Newman Hall of the University of California in Berkeley. On this occasion, the pastor/celebrant came down from the altar to join hands with the student community to pray the Lord's Prayer. In this gesture, people of various roles and races were joined into one to make the whole chapel a sanctuary of praise. This student saw in this gesture a living icon of the Trinity. She saw the church giving full recognition to the uniqueness of its members without compromising their diversity, and she saw that no one person was being made more important than another. She saw in this gesture of the community joined hand to hand before the altar a glimpse of the divine community and the peaceable kingdom of God to which we are all called but which is not yet here in its fullness. To be part of this communal gesture for her was to experience communion in the Spirit of God where everyone exists together as equal partners in Christ. She felt invited into the great dance that goes on at the center of creation bringing all peoples and all creation into one loving union. Such an experience, in turn, provoked in her the moral awareness that when we attend to the world around us and orient ourselves to the needs and concerns of others, we are drawn into the divine life of God. Participating in this living icon was for her an experience of spirituality giving rise to morality, challenging her to re-imagine her everyday ways of being with others.

Feminist Revision

The retrieval of the doctrine of the Trinity in contemporary theology has highlighted the personal and relational aspects of God. This is fertile ground for the contributions of feminist theology to rethink our images of God and to open us to a new awareness of the relation of spirituality to the moral life. Feminist criticism of our God-talk, such as the kind found in Elizabeth Johnson's *She Who Is*,[21] is a protest against the literal interpretation of our images of God and the absolutizing of any one of them. Male images of God, especially the nearly exclusive use of God as father, have come under considerable criticism. While God as the father figure in the sky of our childhood may have been useful to get us to start trying to understand God in personal terms, its nearly exclusive use as an image of God has become an unnecessary stumbling block to faith for many, especially for women.

Celie, in Alice Walker's *The Color Purple*, is an example of what is at stake. She tells her mentor and liberator, Shug Avery, that her God looks just like white men who have dominated her, only bigger. Celie lives with an image of God who has the power to control and dominate her just as the men do who have been part of her life. Shug's advice to Celie is that, if she is ever to find her way to freedom, she will have to get men off her eyeball.[22] Celie has to have her sight restored by removing the cataracts of a racist and sexist culture that gave her only a white male image of God. Celie's life shows how living under the domination of this white male image of God and the patriarchal structure that it supports has managed to instill in her a sense of powerlessness, dependence, and distrust of her own authority, experience, and knowledge. Such a self-perception is no help to Celie, nor would it be to any other woman for that matter, in her quest for adult autonomy, responsibility, and self-respect. What Alice Walker has created in her character, Celie, expresses the experience of many women, and articulates credibly and strongly feminist criticism of the persistent use of male-dominated images for God.

THE CALL TO HOLINESS

Many of our official prayers, documents, and even some preaching keep alive predominantly male images of God, such as *king, lord, master,* and especially *father.* In the history of Western art, the most common depiction of God is that of an old white man with a beard. Michelangelo's image of God the Creator on the ceiling of the Sistine Chapel is a good example. The frequent and familiar usage of male speech and masculine images of God in an uncritically literal way has a significant impact on the religious imagination, and so on the spirituality and morality of women and men. How we experience ourselves in relation to God and to one another is affected by the imputed masculinity of God. The persistent use of masculine images can instill a sense that maleness is an essential character of God, that God is on the side of men, that female images of God are deviant, and that women don't count.

According to feminist theologians Ann Carr and Elizabeth Johnson, the feminist criticism of such an exclusive use of male images for God is that it too easily gives a divine legitimation to patriarchal structures in church, family, and society. Patriarchal patterns (or "father rule") sanction a male-centered worldview where men are in control, women are subordinate to men and seen as property of husbands and fathers, and men possess dignity in contrast to women who are seen as inferior, defective, and less than fully human. Male images of God create the impression that only male power is saving power. This effectively denies to women the possibility of the religious affirmation of their own power and undermines their sense of moral agency and self-respect.[23]

Sandra Schneiders is sympathetic with the feminist criticism of patriarchy supported by the masculine imagery of God, yet she also recognizes that the Bible makes quite clear that the male metaphors are not to be taken literally or made absolute. Feminine images of God in the Bible tell us something very important about God, "something we may well not have discovered for ourselves in a male-dominated community, that God is neither male nor female, that God is both feminine and masculine."[24] For example, for the prophets, the full tenderness of God's care for Israel is best expressed in mother/father images. Hosea describes God as a loving parent who provides the care that would be the task of the mother in Hebrew society (Hos 11:1–4). Second Isaiah (49:15) compares God's care for Israel to a mother's care for her child. Isaiah 66:9–13 designates God as mother, and Jeremiah 31:20 reveals God's motherly compassion. In the wisdom literature, Wisdom is personified as a woman (Prov 1:20 ff.). In the Gospels, Luke's "Lost and Found Department" (Luke 15) depicts God's compassion for the lost both in masculine and feminine images (as shepherd, as a woman searching for a lost coin, and as merciful father).

Schneiders further argues that the father image of God is not used in the Bible to portray God as a patriarch dominating the people or exercising coercive power over them, nor is it used to suggest that the divine parenthood is exclusively paternal. Rather, she contends, "the father metaphor is evoked precisely to describe the compassionate love of God who is like a parent spurned by ungrateful children but who is endless in patience and loving-kindness toward a rebellious people."[25] The God who is presented as a father in the Old Testament is like the father in the New Testament parable of the prodigal son (Luke 15:11–32). In this parable Jesus presents the fatherhood of God as the antithesis of patriarchy. The father in that parable images God as one who renounces the patriarchal privilege to punish the son who rebelled against patriarchy by exercising his autonomy. Rather, God is shown as the one who refuses to own us, demand our submission, or punish our rebellion. According to Schneiders, "God is one who respects our freedom, mourns our alienation, waits patiently for our return, and accepts our love as pure gift."[26]

While the compassionate aspect of the father image of God is secure in the biblical witness of God and can stimulate the moral imagination to respect individual freedom and to treat the other with equal dignity, the overuse of the father image for God must be corrected by using other images available to us from our biblical and theological tradition. A frequently cited example of balancing images of God is found in the work of Julian of Norwich, an English mystic who lived in the last half of the fourteenth century. Her *Revelation of Love* (or *Showings*) records her experience of God. In it she uses the image of God as Mother to describe her experience of both God and Jesus:

> And the Second Person of the Trinity is Mother in nature, in our substantial making, in whom we are grounded and rooted; and he is also our Mother in mercy in taking our sensuality. And so our Mother works in diverse ways for us, so that our parts are held together. For in our Mother Christ we profit and increase as in mercy he reforms and restores us,

while, by the power of his passion and his death and rising, he ones us to our substance. And so our Mother works in such a merciful way with all his children, making them buxom and obedient.[27]

Julian's ability to juxtapose both male and female images of God makes it clear that God transcends sexuality and gives equal dignity to the holiness and experience of men and women. Exclusively male imagery is simply inadequate to express the reality of God across the full range of our tradition and within women's own experience.

Feminist theologian Sallie McFague proposes three other images of God that have biblical warrant: God as Mother, Lover, and Friend.[28] She shows how each of her models entails an ethic that participates in God's dynamic presence in the world. God as Mother expresses the creative activity of God as an act of giving birth. By underscoring God's closeness to us, this image engenders an ethic of justice as caring that all forms of life may prosper. God as Lover implies the saving activity of God who takes pleasure in all that is, finds it valuable, and delights in its fulfillment. This image engenders an ethics of healing that restores wholeness where there has been division and seeks a balanced integration of all aspects of creation. God as Friend implies the sustaining activity of God who cares for the well-being of all the Earth. This image engenders an ethics of companionship that is inclusive of all and where all join in mutual responsibility for the well-being of the world. In McFague's images of God, the universe and God are neither totally distant nor totally different. In her images we have a more sacred planet and a more involved

God. Experiences of God expressed in her images already involve us in responsibility for one another and for the Earth. In this way, spirituality gives rise to morality.

Conclusion

In summary, then, this chapter has explored the conviction that experiencing God with faith stands at the center of spirituality and morality. Images of God express and shape that experience and open us to the moral dimensions of our spiritual experience. The incomprehensible reality of God requires that we alternate our images of God lest we take any one image as the total reality of God. Likewise, to be a responsible Christian with an adult spirituality requires that one be contemplative. This does not mean that we should run into the desert and seek isolated solitude; but rather, we must live with an awareness of God and seek deeper communion with God. Karl Rahner was convinced that the future of Christianity depends on its ability to bring the ordinary believer to an appreciation of the presence of God in everyday experiences:

> The Christian of the future will be a mystic or he will not exist at all. If by mysticism we mean, not singular parapsychological phenomena, but a genuine experience of God emerging from the very heart of our existence, this statement is very true and its truth and importance will become still clearer in the spirituality of the future.[29]

What he means is that the ultimate decision of faith comes not from instruction, nor from rational argument, nor from the support of public opinion. It comes, rather, from the personal experience of God at the very heart of daily life. Spirituality and morality cannot be kept alive by external helps but only through a personal experience of God in the Holy Spirit. The interrelationship of spirituality and morality calls us to attend to the mystery of God already present in our life. When we attend to God, we feel the moral tug to care about what God cares about. Our response is our morality giving public expression to our spirituality.

❖

These first four chapters have laid the foundation for making the connection between spirituality and the moral life. In brief, the grounding conviction of these chapters is that an "experience of God" is the common point of reference for spirituality and morality. Spirituality fundamentally has to do with one's experience of God and the moral life is our response to God. So whether we experience God at all or how we experience God ought to make a difference for the moral life. The roots of morality (responding to God) lie in spirituality (experience of God), and the fruits of spirituality can be found in the moral life.

These chapters have tried to show that spirituality and morality are inseparably connected. Historically, however, we have not always treated them that way. Moral theology went its own way when it became preoccupied with determining which actions were sins or not and with resolving conflicts of obligations according to the objective principles of natural law. This focus for morality generated a close alliance with canon law. The Bible, and especially the person of Jesus, played a role in devotional life, but they were, for the most part, merely a footnote in moral theology. Christian religious experience and personal growth in faith were the preserve of ascetical theology.

The second half of the twentieth century, however, witnessed a monumental renewal of moral theology, which was rooted in the Bible and integrated with the great mysteries of faith. It focused on the total human vocation of living in response to God's self-communication to us in creation, in history, and most fully in Jesus. This has been a key insight in appreciating how spirituality is related to the moral life. No longer is morality considered to be principally a matter of obeying laws. Rather, it engages the discerning heart guided by the Holy Spirit to search for what God's offer of divine love enables us to be and to do. This broader vision for morality puts a significant emphasis on the inner personal dynamics of the moral life that are the interests of virtue ethics.

The retrieval of character and virtue in moral theology has become a promising avenue for appreciating the link between spirituality and the moral life. Virtue ethics and spirituality both share the common conviction that the person lives as an integrated whole with the body connecting to the inner spirit through the instruments of the soul, especially the emotions and the imagination. To round out this picture of the relationship of spirituality to the moral life, we consider in the next chapters how spiritual practices also play a formative role in shaping the person's character and virtue. We turn then to the role of practices and life in the Spirit.

PART III

❖

Practicing the Faith

5.

Practices: Spiritual and Moral

❖

Are you a *practicing* Catholic? Does this question sound familiar? We answer that question by pointing to our regular participation in certain practices that express Catholic identity. Minimally, to be a "practicing" Catholic means keeping the precepts of the church: to attend Mass on Sunday and holy days of obligation; to confess once a year; to receive Eucharist during Easter time; to observe the days of fast and abstinence; and to contribute to the material needs of the church. These practices, decreed by church authorities, stipulate the minimum of spiritual and moral effort needed for us to grow in our love for God and neighbor. Beyond these minimal requirements, a "practicing" Catholic may also do a number of other things: pray privately, make a retreat, say the rosary; attend Benediction; make the Stations of the Cross; say litanies and make novenas; recite the Divine Office (Liturgy of the Hours); go to Mass on first Fridays; use sacramentals like holy water, medals, and statues; make a pilgrimage to various shrines like Fatima or Lourdes; and, in more recent years, read the Bible and try to guide one's life by it, and contribute to the promotion of social justice. All of this shows that we cannot fully explain what it means to be Catholic without referring to its characteristic practices, both spiritual and moral. Our practices show the face of our tradition to the world.

Encouraging practices such as these, and minimally requiring some, is one way the church has provided opportunities for us to deepen our spiritual lives and to nourish and shape our moral lives. While the previous chapters have shown a very broad interest in spirituality and the moral life and only hinted at some practices, this chapter narrows our interest to the practices of prayer and eucharistic worship and their implications for the moral life. The underlying conviction here is that if practices like these do not lead to the moral life, then our spirituality is like an incomplete sentence. Spiritual practices should bring us to a heightened sensitivity to our moral responsibilities, and moral living should return us to our spiritual practices where we focus ourselves on our ultimate dependence on God. To deal with spiritual and moral practices in this reciprocal way affirms the inseparability of the love of God and love of neighbor. But first a word about the notion of spiritual practices and their transforming effect on the moral life.

Spiritual Practices

An interest in "practices" has been growing recently among philosophers, theologians, ethicists, and social scientists.[1] Sociologist Robert Wuthnow's *After Heaven: Spirituality in America Since the 1950s*[2] gives us a helpful typology of spirituality in America that best situates the interests of this chapter. He distinguishes three types of spirituality. A spirituality of *dwelling* characterized the '50s. We went to church and followed the rules. Our religious affiliation provided a stable sense of place and familiar ways to worship God amidst growing uncertainties in the world. In the '60s and '70s, a spirituality of *seeking* emerged as Americans sought their own way to the sacred beyond the confines of the sacred space and traditions of the established churches. It offered greater freedom for people to fill themselves with a variety of religious experiences, but they were not being nourished by the depth of any one tradition. These were the decades that gave us people who claimed that they were spiritual but not religious. The third type, a spirituality of *practices*, has emerged to provide discipline, focus, and depth to one's spiritual quest. They usually consist in some form of talking to God, listening to God, or simply being in the presence of God. Devotional activities such as prayer, inspirational reading, meditating on the Bible, and participating in eucharistic worship are intentional activities integrated into ordinary life that provide the discipline the seekers lacked and the depth the dwellers took for granted. Practice-oriented spirituality emphasizes the discipline of setting off a "sacred" space and setting aside a special time on a regular basis in order to cultivate one's relationship with God, even though both the time and space remain negotiable. For example, it doesn't always have to be in a church or on Sunday that we do the practice. These practices have depth when nurtured by practice-oriented religious organizations that ground the practice in a tradition of faith.

As we saw, the spiritual life is born in desire—a desire for wholeness, for meaning, for connection, for God. Christian spirituality grows as we attend to God's love for us and respond to God's word for us in Christ. But to be addressed by God we need an "address," which spiritual practices provide. Thanks to spiritual practices we can be at home for God by creating a space so that God can be with us and we can be with God. The devotional manuals of the great spiritual writers recognize that the way to nurture one's religious self is *not* through ideas and arguments that aim at insight into God. Rather, it is through the regular exercise of practices, such as prayer, fasting, physical work, making reparations, and self-denying service to others, that we cumulatively open a receptive space for God.[3] Practices provide the space where we can receive God and develop a lifestyle that reflects an awareness of living in the presence of God. Through the practices we learn how to shape our lives around Christian attitudes and values. In brief, then, a spiritual practice is an intentional, soulful, and somatic activity done on a regular basis in order to strengthen one's relationship to God or to become more fully aware of God's presence.

The operative terms of reference for understanding a spiritual practice are *intentional* and *God*. As "intentional," a spiritual practice assumes a deliberate, soulful effort to develop one's awareness of God and response to God. As intentional, we do it with soul. Inspired by the deep desire of the human spirit, we engage in practices with an openness to be moved by the Spirit working in and through them. An intentional practice is not an occasional burst of enthusiasm (I'm feeling pious today), nor a dutiful following of the law (The church requires it), nor a coerced caving in to social pressure (My parents make me do it), nor a social propriety (It looks good and everyone is doing it). Rather, an intentional spiritual practice is a personally committed exercise that we set time aside to do regularly and purposefully, like going to church on Sunday or taking fifteen minutes of quiet time each morning.

To say that a spiritual practice is "intentional" is not to dismiss any role whatsoever for "rote participation" in the process of acquiring the practice. After all, we come to see the worth of what we do only gradually. What begins as an unreflective pattern of going along with parental pressure, for example, can eventually become a committed practice. This is what makes acquiring a practice to be like acquiring a virtue. Neither happens automatically. Practices and virtues must be honed over time. They require having opportunities to engage in the activity frequently and to have one's commitment to it reinforced by others whom we admire and whom we can observe and imitate in doing the practice. So, it would not be surprising to learn that most of our religious practices began as rote participation.

For example, in the beginning, we go along with what our family does. Since going to Mass on Sunday is a family practice, then as children we start going to Mass. We do so simply because we are members of the family and not because we are committed to the meaning of the Eucharist. The Mass may very well remain just a ritual for a long time. Eventually, the habit of regularly attending Mass can open us to the realization that we are related to God and that God cares for us. Rote participation in the religious practice provides the experiential base for catching its meaning later when we are more receptive to it.[4]

These dynamics of participation inform the advice Archbishop Rembert Weakland gives to young people who are having a difficult time understanding what it means to be Catholic. Before talking about what it means to be Catholic, he tells them that, for six months, they are to participate in Mass weekly with the same congregation and, at the same time, work in a soup kitchen for the poor. The rhythm of spiritual and moral practices—common prayer and service—will give them the basis for understanding what it means to be Catholic.[5] Notice, he doesn't privilege the intellect by giving them anything to read at first, not the Catechism, not encyclicals, not even Rahner. He tells them rather to practice the faith before they try to interpret it. The underlying conviction of this advice is that we get to the meaning of our faith through the body before we grasp it with the mind. In rituals we experience what we believe, because practices (spiritual and moral) are ways we embody our faith. Engaging in the practice makes it possible for God's Word to enter our hearts. The practice becomes a physical way to express our spirit's reaching out to God and a physical space for God's Spirit to act on our soul.

In addition to *intentional*, the other operative term in our understanding of a spiritual practice is *God*. The practices' orientation to God helps us understand why we do them in the first place. We do them to open ourselves to God's love, to show our love for God, and to deepen our relationship with God. We do not engage in practices to improve our life, health, or relationships. We practice the faith to be true to our spiritual nature that hungers for God. While spiritual practices may have a moral dimension inherent in them that contributes to fostering moral practices, like the virtues, this formative element is an indirect effect of the spiritual practice. The practice is not simply a preparation for loving our neighbor or for improving ourselves. The true purpose of the spiritual practice is to worship God, to show our love for God, and to deepen our awareness of and relationship to God. William Spohn is emphatic on this point: "If the intent of worship is not God but personal growth, then God is being reduced to a means, which is a form of idolatry."[6]

While maintaining the priority of spiritual practices to strengthen one's relationship to God, Christian morality is also interested in drawing out the moral dimensions inherent in them. Ethical reflection on practicing the faith shows us how moral practices and character formation are inherent in spiritual practices. We have some indications of these moral dimensions in those interviewed by Robert Wuthnow. In Avery Fielding's case, for example, spiritual practices nurtured a loving perspective. She explains,

> Of the things that I learned as a child was to be judgmental and critical. So through my own spirituality I have really worked hard at undoing that: to learn not to pass judgment on what I see because I don't see the whole picture, to not be critical of people or places or things but to see it from a more loving perspective.[7]

Wuthnow goes on to explain how the reflection that accompanies the practice-informed spirituality helped Avery Fielding understand her own biases and interests and became the occasion to remind her of the larger moral perspective that spirituality entails.

Avery Fielding's story illustrates how spiritual practices can be life transforming to the extent that they enable us to see life differently. We may notice things we haven't noticed before because we acquire a capacity to take in more. But we also see what everyone sees but in a different way. That's the way it also is for Lydia Garcia in Robert Wuthnow's book, *Creative Spirituality*. Lydia is an artist in New Mexico who integrates her spirituality into her painting of *santos* and *retablos*. Her daily prayer and participation in Mass give her a larger sense of the universe. "Things don't change, she reflects, but you see them differently."[8] This new seeing is a spiritual perspective. That is, we see everything in its relation to God.

Similarly, Coleman McGregor's spiritual practices engender the moral practices of developing his relationship to God and of deepening his commitment to helping others. For example, he has long been drawn to charitable activities, but his devotion to God has changed how he understands this commitment. He elaborates,

> Working at soup kitchens and making baskets for the poor are all good projects,…but I think you need to do it out of the experience of being so deeply loved yourself that you want to give it back. When you are deeply loved by God, you want to return it.…I don't believe we are given what we have to hold to ourselves. I think part of what the circle of life is about is to share what you have, to give what you have, to be part of salvation history, to build a better world.[9]

Avery Fielding and Coleman McGregor both illustrate how spending time cultivating our relationship with God can free us from our self-interested pursuits so that we can focus on the needs of others. The same is true for the artists Wuthnow interviews for his study of art as a spiritual practice in *Creative Spirituality*:

> Spiritual practice reinforces these artists' commitment to serve others by regularly focusing their attention on questions about what matters in life. They become more aware that self-gratification is not the ultimate aim of their work and that they participate through their work in human and even cosmic forces they cannot control. They nevertheless recognize that they play an active part in creating goodness and beauty.[10]

Spiritual practices become life transforming to the extent that they help us to see differently and to behave differently. Even though we may not always be able to change what we see, seeing it differently helps us to respond differently. Perception, remember, informs moral judgments. Once we see the stranger as neighbor in need, we might respond differently. Spiritual practices open us to see and judge all things in relation to our experience of God and our commitment to care about what God cares about.

A strong note of caution must be sounded here about spiritual practices as life-transforming activities. The caution: Nothing is automatic! There is no guarantee that if we do the practices then we will acquire a certain character or behave in a certain way. Look around. Do all those you know who "practice" their faith have the same attitude or act in the same way? Clearly not. So we must be careful about claiming too much for the transforming potential of our spiritual practices. If we do, we risk creating a theological version of *Field of Dreams*. Remember, in the motion picture of that title the motivation to build the baseball field is the advice, "If you build it, they will come." The theological version would be, "If you practice your faith, you will be transformed." This is not necessarily so. There is no guarantee. This is not Hollywood. The link is not so automatic.

The connections between spiritual practices and the moral life are complex, not simple. While spiritual practices can keep alive our relationship to God and our way of seeing all things in relation to God, it takes practical moral decisions and the habit of moral practices to implement our spiritual relationship and vision. Moreover, since our personal and cultural experiences are also at stake in determining moral character and choice, spiritual practices do not have a monopoly on our morality. Given the many factors that influence our moral development and given the fact that not everyone engages common practices with the same depth of commitment to their meaning, we cannot expect practices to ensure a certain kind of moral character and behavior.

Graham Greene's novel *A Burnt-Out Case* provides a good illustration of how moral practices can outrun spiritual ones. In this story, an order of priests and sisters runs a leprosarium in Africa. Working for them are two men who do not share their religious vision or spiritual practices. Querry considers himself a "retired Catholic." He has not been to Mass for more than twenty years. Dr. Colin has long since lost his faith in any god the priests and sisters would be able to recognize. The priests and sisters carry on with their spiritual practice of regular Mass and Divine Office. Querry and Dr. Colin have given up praying long ago. Yet these two men, and not the priests and sisters, are the greater models of humility and unselfishness in the way they care for others.

Many factors influence our character and behavior. Although they are not alone in influencing our morality, spiritual practices nevertheless carry a rich potential for changing our moral life when we engage them with the right intention and with deep commitment. While we can say that our love for God expressed through our practices can and ought to lead to loving what God loves, the causal connection is not inevitable. We misunderstand our finitude and our freedom, along with the multiple influences on our character, if we think that loving God makes us lovers of the world. While loving God can incline us to love others, there is no easy and sure connection between loving God, loving our neighbor, and loving ourselves.

Given this word of caution that practices do not guarantee moral transformation, the rest of this chapter is interested in the link to moral practices that is possible when we engage prayer and eucharistic worship with the right intention to love God.

Prayer

Prayer is any act that expresses in word or gesture our desire to be in the presence of God, to deepen our awareness of God, and to strengthen our relationship to God. It is the most obvious practice to identify one's spirituality. For prayer embodies the central conviction of Christian spirituality, namely, that we are in a personal relation to God and that this relationship truly affects our lives.[11]

Given such a broad understanding of prayer, there is a sense in which we can say that our lives themselves are a form of prayer. Since God is at the depths of every act and the Spirit of God is walking with us through the day, the very business of living expresses our relationship to God. But we do not consciously connect to God in every mundane thing we do. Cultivating the habit of focused moments of prayer provides a place for God to meet us and for us consciously to connect with God. In prayer we pay attention to God more carefully, perhaps, than anywhere else. As chapter 6 will show, prayer is the proper context for discerning actions that fit our commitment to God. Through prayer, we polish the lenses of our "God glasses" to see more clearly everything in relation to God. Taking on this perspective can make us more readily express thanks for simple gifts, like the food we have to eat and the friends we have to enjoy. Prayer can help make us ready to ask forgiveness when we grow careless, or speak a word of encouraging affirmation to someone in need. As the next chapter will show, prayer can also help us to discern actions that fit our commitment to God. To the extent that we pray, we open ourselves to becoming more virtuous, to deepening our awareness of the mystery of God's presence in the midst of our life, and to enriching our appreciation of life as a gift of God.

Prayer is born in desire. Sebastian Moore is a good guide to human desire. He suggests that the desire to be desired ("I want you. Do you want me?") is the persistent longing of the human spirit.[12] Or, as John Shea puts it, "When we kiss, we want to be kissed back."[13] This human hunger to love and to be loved makes us naturally spiritual and gives rise to prayer forms of all sorts. No matter what the form, the true direction of prayer is always toward God in love, praise, and thanksgiving. We pray to express our love for God and to deepen our affective relationship to God. Our growing oneness with God entails a solidarity with the world, because by loving God in a more committed way, we begin to see the world and our neighbors from the perspective of God's care for all things.

If it is true that we respond to what we see, then when we begin to see all things within the horizon of God, we can begin to respond to them as reflections of God. This is how our spirituality influences the moral life. Perhaps an example can help. Remember Mary Jane from chapter 1, the one who followed the spiritual practice of taking quiet time each morning before she went to work? On some days, she prays with scripture; on other days, she prays for those at work. Sometimes she prays through her anticipated appointments for the day; and sometimes she just sits there in quiet. In whatever form she prays, she believes that she is in the presence of God whose Spirit is at work not only in all these forms of prayer but also in her day, making things turn out for good.

From the Bible, Mary Jane knows that God will come to her in the surprises that will happen during the day. She leaves her prayer open to the unexpected and with a sense of humor that will catch the incongruous as an epiphany of grace. From her prayers of intercession, she feels empathy for those who will intersect her life that day. She is ready with a word of encouragement and affirmation that is just right for each one. Her intercessory prayer sets her up to be a blessing for them rather than a judgment. From her appointment book, she sees each meeting as a time when God's Spirit will be at work bringing people into cooperative communion with one another. She does not put people on edge worrying that they might slip up. From her quiet time, she takes an open and receptive heart, a warmth and a graciousness that is ready to listen and to learn.

Mary Jane is an example of how the formation of character and actions are a side effect of her daily spiritual practice of deepening her commitment to God. She does not pray so as to become humble, grateful, trusting, or caring. She prays principally to deepen her relationship with God and to express her love for God. But her virtues and actions arise from trying to live out of a life centered on God and from a perspective fashioned by her convictions about God's presence and action in the world.

To give a sense of how the practice of prayer is related to the moral life, I will examine three common forms of prayer: vocal prayer of petition and intercession, mental prayer of meditation on scripture, and communal, ritual prayer of eucharistic worship.

Petition and Intercession

Petitionary prayer brings before God the needs of the one making the prayer. The distorted form of this prayer can too easily be reduced to a "gimme prayer" that is like a business proposition with God that asks: What do I get out of it? With its focus on what God cares about, the Lord's Prayer is the better model for such prayer, with its series of petitions beginning with "Your Kingdom come" and ending with "Deliver us from evil." Intercessory prayer, by contrast, brings before God the needs of others. In the form of either petition or intercession, desire, dependence, and determination constitute the inner dynamics of the practice of prayer. Out of desire for God we recognize what we need if we are to rest in God. So we pray for health, for peace, for a passing grade, for forgiveness, and for whatever else will bring us to the fullness of life in union with God.

The desire for forgiveness is what drives Ian Bedloe to pray in Ann Tyler's *Saint Maybe*.[14] The novel begins with Ian at age seventeen. His family occasionally attends the Presbyterian Church where worship is quite formal, and prayer is done by the book. At seventeen, Ian has little interest in church or in things religious, but then all that changes. In a moment of anger and frustration, Ian tells his brother Danny that Danny's wife, Lucy, has been unfaithful. She hadn't been, but Ian didn't know that at the time. Immediately after Ian's outburst of anger, Danny drives his car into a wall and kills himself. A few months later, Lucy takes an overdose of sleeping pills to kill herself. Tormented by guilt, Ian seeks forgiveness. One evening, he passes a storefront church and is drawn to the sound of hymn singing and the neon sign proclaiming the Church of the Second Chance. Ian enters just as the small congregation begins to pray. The minister, unlike the Presbyterian pastor, does not use a prayer book. He invites the congregation to offer their own petitions and intercessions. The worshipers pray for sick friends and for each other. Ian prays for forgiveness, his greatest need for now.

Prayers of petition and intercession say, in effect, that we are not self-sufficient and that we are not alone. Because we are not self-sufficient, these prayers require an attitude of dependence on God who is the source and sustainer of all. Prayer as dependence makes it possible for us to accept the most difficult proposition in the world—that there is but one God and no more than that! This is the very awareness that came to the retreatant who sat all night in the silent chapel waiting to hear God's word for her life. She left with a single awareness that changed her life. The word she heard was "I'm God, you're not."

In prayer, we come before God as creatures who must surrender our need to be in absolute control and accept our reliance upon others, upon families and friends, upon social structures and processes, upon culture, and upon the continuities in nature. According to Karl Rahner's theology of prayer, these human experiences of dependence open us to our ultimate dependence on God. Praying in faith and in love relativizes our dominion and control, and it opens us to surrender to God's universal will for salvation. If prayer were another instrument for getting things done, then it would not be far from magic. For Rahner, we cannot properly come to God in petition without first giving ourselves in trusting submission to God with the same attitude of Jesus before his death: Let your will be done, not mine. Otherwise, our petition is not really a prayer at all but an attempt to influence God as if by some magical conjuration.[15]

The regular practice of prayer can, in time, strengthen our virtue to be patient with the pace at which life unfolds because we live with hope that all will be well, and we grow more grateful because we believe that all things are under the care of God. In prayer, we learn to see with the eyes of our heart and so gain new insight into God or a greater sensitivity to the presence of God in our midst. What seems to others like coincidence, luck, or mere human effort to others is for us the hand of God at work. As this becomes our habitual way of seeing the world, we acquire a discerning heart with a felt awareness of God's presence and of what stands in the way of God, such as injustice and exploitation. As we draw closer to God and become more sensitive to what opposes God, we gain a compassion that includes more and more people. Our moral lives take on a different tone and quality as we become more aware of others and committed to caring for one another and for the world. We cannot pray authentically without at the same time working to set right the unjust conditions in society.

Intercessory prayer especially requires that our hearts be open to the world in solidarity with the needs and hopes of others. For Dietrich Bonhoeffer, intercessory prayer is at the heart of life together:

> A Christian community either lives by the intercessory prayers of its members for one another, or the community will be destroyed. I can no longer condemn or hate other Christians for whom I pray, no matter how much trouble they cause me.[16]

The practice of this form of prayer deepens and strengthens our relationship with God and those with whom we live and for whom we pray. In prayers of intercession, the one who prays identifies with others and is formed in empathy and compassion.

As Bonhoeffer sees it, "As far as we are concerned, there is no dislike, no personal tension, no disunity or strife, that cannot be overcome by intercessory prayer."[17]

At least that is what Ian Bedloe felt when he prayed with the community of the Church of the Second Chance. After each prayer, the community would pause in silence so that each worshiper could extend the prayer on his or her own. Ian voiced his prayer for forgiveness, and then, in the silence that followed, floated on the prayers that he didn't hear, but felt from the community. The prayers that surrounded and sustained Ian were the prayers being offered by others. He knew his solidarity with them and could feel their empathy with him.

Unfortunately, we do not always pray this way. Sometimes we just go through the motions. We pray to fulfill a duty. We say our prayers, and so get them done. But our hearts are not in them. In such soulless prayer, we are not at home for God to "address" us. Then, too, instead of praying out of an attitude of dependence and solidarity, we sometimes pray out of self-centered hearts. Self-centered prayers approach God as a means to our own ends, as though God's whole purpose is to fulfill our needs. These are not prayers of faith but of manipulation. Self-centered "gimme prayers" seek to control and dominate, as though these prayers could cause God to respond according to our designs. In effect, they seek to employ God for our service. Petitions become orders for God to give us our way, and intercessions become strategies on how we want it done.

Prayers of faith and trust, however, express a desire to deepen our relationship with God and to see ourselves and all things under the care of God. We pray in the first place because we believe that God is present and active in the world and cares for the well-being of all. In prayers of faith and trust, God is petitioned, not controlled. These prayers place all things under the care of God and express the unity and mutual care that bind us to one another.

Petitions and intercessions are not for passive souls. These prayers are not attempts to escape social responsibility by turning over to God what we want nothing to do with. Rather, prayers of faith and trust lead us toward God in love and gratitude and, in so doing, they also lead us toward the loving service that expresses our interdependence with others and creation. To pray with the formula "in and through Christ" is to pray through the whole Body of Christ, which includes us. Remember, God comes to us through us. This is the way of the incarnation. So in our petitions and intercessions, we are doing more than asking God to intervene. We are also committing ourselves to assume responsibility to bring about that for which we pray. That is to say, our prayers have a self-involving character to them, which is the inner dynamic of determination. This is not just the determination of shamelessly persisting in our petition, it is even more the determination to live into that for which we pray.

As we saw, Ian prayed for forgiveness. But much to his surprise, his prayer did not stop there. After the service in which he voiced his petition, the minister asks him if he had had a response to his prayer. Ian thinks the minister will assure him of forgiveness and his guilt will be over. But the minister tells him, in effect, that his prayer is only beginning. In fact, his prayer moves him into assuming responsibility for Danny's and Lucy's children. His determination to care for them completes his prayer. Praying for forgiveness does not get him off the hook of doing the love that is the desire of the prayer in the first place.

It is so in our prayer, too. If we pray for health, it is not so that we can continue to live a self-centered life. It means doing what we can to take care of ourselves so that we can use our gifts to enrich life for everyone. If we pray to pass an exam, it is not to avoid shame. It is to study so that our learning will enable us to serve others competently. If we pray for peace, it is not so that we can simply avoid conflicts. It is so that we can forgive those who have hurt us and become instruments of reconciliation wherever we are. If we pray for our friend who is depressed, but do not speak to her or encourage her, then we are not praying "in Christ" in the fullest sense. Prayers of faith and trust express our desire to deepen our relationship to God in Christ and to live in love with one another and with the whole world. These prayers express our spirituality and give direction to our moral life.

Praying with Scripture

The Bible is a privileged source of inspired stories and images of encounters with God. When we use the Bible in prayer, we count on its being a privileged context for our encountering God as well. We use the Bible in prayer not so much as a window into the past, but as a mirror reflecting our way of relating to God today. The mirroring power of the biblical story helps us to see more clearly the movements of grace in our life. Scripture as mirror offers back to us what we did not know was there.

Reflected in the scripture is the very stuff that makes us who we are—our desires and disappointments, our hopes and our hurts, our loves and our longings, our pride and our prejudice, and even more, what we did not even expect or suspect, God's all-embracing love. Herein lies the morally formative power of this kind of prayer. By engaging our imaginations in praying with scripture, we cross the bridge between the biblical texts of encounters with God in the past and the newly graced person we can become with the character and virtues needed to live in the Spirit of God today.

Using the imagination in prayer with the Bible is an ancient form of meditation and contemplation. But *meditation* and *contemplation,* like *mystic* and *mystical,* have become bruised terms in our vocabulary of spirituality. They can have esoteric meanings, suggesting that meditation is more of a thinking process and contemplation more of a receptive, heart response meant only for those who are more advanced in the spiritual life. But there is also a widely accepted understanding of them that is much simpler and makes this prayer form more accessible to everyone in the church. This simpler understanding is that biblical meditation or contemplation uses the Bible as imaginative literature. That is, we turn to the stories of the Bible for soul food. As such, the Bible is not primarily a source for historical information or even a resource for making arguments about God. The Bible, rather, bears witness to God through its stories and images that express encounters with God. The imagination sees with eyes rooted in the heart. For this reason, using the imagination in prayer with scripture is not an intellectual grasping of concepts about God or Jesus, but rather a playful interacting of the text and our experience. This playful interaction is the medium of a personal encounter with God and Jesus that can stir our hearts with responses of faith, hope, and love.

The imagination played a significant role in the monastic practice of *lectio divina*. This is the practice of reading the Bible with a listening heart in such a way that we enter a dialogue in which God speaks to us through the text. We read the text slowly and stop when we are struck by a word *(mercy, fear, go)*, a phrase ("Come and see," "Whom do you seek?"), or an image (the lame walking, disciples following, catching fish, breaking bread). We believe that these are ways that God is speaking to us in our prayer. Our part in the dialogue is to stop reading at this point and to savor what we hear by repeating slowly what strikes us. This is our way of resting in God's presence to us at the moment. Our response in the dialogue comes from listening to what is rising from our hearts. We incorporate what we feel and hear into our moral life by way of nurturing a new attitude (such as gratitude, compassion, and forgiveness) and acting in a way that expresses this interior disposition (by saying "Thanks" for a favor received, by spending time with a sick friend, and by learning to say "I'm sorry"). In these ways we deepen our commitment to live in the Spirit of God.[18]

Another way we can engage the imagination in praying with the Bible is in a form of Ignatian contemplation.[19] Simply put, this is recreating the biblical scene in our imagination and then taking part in the action in order to make it present to us. In this practice, the biblical story becomes the environment we live in for that moment of prayer. When we recognize ourselves within its world, it opens for us new understandings of ourselves and new possibilities for our discipleship. The biblical story stands before us not primarily as a source of information about God and the Lord Jesus, but more immediately as an invitation calling us to participate in a living relationship with God. Just as we bring our questions and concerns to the biblical stories, so we let the questions and concerns of the stories address us. "Whom do you say I am?" "What do you want me to do for you?" and "Whom do you seek?" are questions addressed not just to disciples of the past, but also to us today. "Do not let your hearts be troubled" is spoken to all disciples, both then and now. The story starts the conversation, and then we take it in different directions. To do this we must first get inside the drama by imaginatively entering into the scene and experiencing the feelings appropriate to it. This step in prayer is aided by taking on the role of one of the characters and even by assuming in our body posture or by gesture the mood and stance of the character, and then engaging the dialogue so that the questions, concerns, challenges, and affirmations of the text become our own.

When we pray with the Bible this way, the meaning of the story is determined not only by what is there, but also by what we bring to it from our lives. Then the dead daughter of Jairus becomes the child within us that has died and is brought to life again; the adultery forgiven by Jesus is our own infidelities that are forgiven; the road to Emmaus becomes our own journey from despair to hope; Jesus' saying not to worry about food and clothes speaks to all that disturbs our life today. We walk around inside the story with our own experiences so that we can come back to our own lives with a new awareness, attitude, and commitment informed by the encounter with God and the Lord Jesus. For example, to move from focusing on the temptations of Jesus to our own temptations is not to entertain a distraction, but is part of this kind of prayer. When we look at the tempted Jesus being faithful to his Father and his mission by affirming before the glamour of evil that he belonged to God and would be led only by the word of God, then we may be brought face to face with our own temptations to use our power to manipulate others, to be sensational, to be unfaithful, or whatever else our temptations might be. This is our spirituality informing our morality. In our prayer, we move from the past of the story only to be more alert to the present in our lives and open to the future possibilities of ways of being a disciple today. Through the practice of praying with scripture, biblical images can direct our emotions and open our hearts to new levels of sensitivity so that we are disposed to respond in a manner that is in harmony with the story of Jesus.

Here are a few steps for praying with the Bible by means of the imagination in order to engage the world of the story with our own experience.

1. Begin with a prayer asking God to meet you in this prayer, then read the text slowly in order to feel the multiple dimensions of the story.
2. Now imaginatively construct the scene to become aware of the mood of the setting and the feelings of the characters.

3. Cross over into the scene and allow your own feelings and experiences to become part of it. Ask yourself, "Where am I in this scene?"
4. Notice what happens to you when you are addressed. What do you say in return?
5. Close your prayer by asking for the grace you have experienced in this prayer to become real in your life. "Lord, my greatest desire now is..."

In praying with the Bible this way, we are not out to know the text better or to get more information about God. Rather, this practice of prayer treats the Bible as an invitation to meet God and to turn back to God. Through this prayer we can become more aware of God's presence within us and around us and relate to all things in their relation to God.

Praying with the imagination this way also reinforces the association of certain images with the emotions that accompany them and the actions that flow from them. Remember, moral arguments are usually not sufficient to move us to action. Knowing what is right does not guarantee that we will do what is right. We need to be moved. We need some inspirational force to arouse our desire for goodness, to give us courage, or to fire our passion for what is right. Recalling these images in the future disposes us to feel what we felt before. These feelings evoke acting in certain ways.

Timothy O'Connell uses an insight from neurobiologist Antonio Damasio to explain how images are stored in association with emotions that dispose us to feel and act in a certain way. That is why recalling certain experiences from the past (the death of a parent) evokes a particular emotion (sadness) and why certain emotions (happiness) can call forth memories (walking on the beach). O'Connell explains:

> First come the experiences that comprise all of our lives. Associated with these experiences are feelings, including the biochemical components of feelings that we have discussed. Then the experiences are remembered, stored in the brain as images that match the initial experiences. At later moments the memory "reappears" in the brain, an image of tremendous clarity. And when it does, the image generates the same electrochemical reactions as did the initial experience. Thus the feelings are felt once again. Damasio refers to these images as "dispositional representations." That is, they are representations that tend to "dispose" us to experience once again the particular feelings that were associated with previous experiences.[20]

Praying with the scripture, for example, can reinforce religious images and their associated emotions to dispose us to act in certain ways. For instance, the image of the woman caught in adultery may come to mind with the first stirrings of self-righteousness and the desire to condemn another's sin. The image has the power to transform condemnation into forgiveness. Or, when we see a field of flowers, we may feel the comfort of God's care for us and be less anxious.

This practice of prayer, then, can inform the moral life by schooling the emotions so that we are drawn to care about what disciples ought to care about, and by nudging us closer to seeing from God's point of view. Together these biblical images and the emotions that accompany them, along with the emerging images of ourselves in dynamic ways, can serve as guides to discovering new ways of living that would be faithful to what discipleship demands for today.

We move from praying with the biblical story to living the moral life that harmonizes with it by means of the analogical imagination. William Spohn has developed this process at great length.[21] The analogical imagination helps us avoid confusing the following or imitation of Christ with simple mimicry. Mimicry replicates external behavior. It wants to copy Jesus point for point. But this only ignores the historically conditioned nature of Jesus and the texts that reveal him to us. To deny that Jesus was historically conditioned and culturally bound would be to deny that he was an historical figure, a first-century Palestinian Jew. As such, he was neither a product of nor subject to the realities and demands that we have to face today. The texts that reveal him to us reflect these same historically limiting conditions. Imitation, or the following of Christ as a disciple, respects the difference between then and now and seeks to catch the spirit of Jesus for today. This is the goal of the analogical imagination.

For example, the way Jesus led the community of his followers was as a "servant leader." In the Gospel of Matthew, Jesus instructed his disciples not to broaden their phylacteries or to lengthen their tassels, not to take the reserved seats in the religious assembly, nor to use titles, such as "rabbi," "father," or "instructors" (Matt 23:5–10). In other words, they were to avoid all techniques that would secure positions of superiority in their communities, that would attract attention, or that would require others to grant them the status of superiority. If this is how we are to serve in the imitation of Christ, then what do we do when we are heads of households, pastors of parishes, employers in corporations, are singled out for recognition or given titles of honor? His words are applicable today when applied analogously. The challenge to the moral life is to be faithful and creative at the same time. So, analogously, we look for ways to serve that do not dominate. Just as Jesus was present to others with a special concern for those who were vulnerable, so, analogously, we look for ways to be as inclusive in spirit and as healing in deed as he was to those who are the least, the last, and the lost of our day.

Using our imaginations in prayer like this sharpens our moral awareness. The moral life, after all, is about more than making decisions and engaging in moral actions. It is also about coming to a truthful vision of ourselves, others, and the world.[22] As we engage new images, we get access to new lenses for our "God glasses." We begin to see the presence of God in more and more places in our life and hear the call of God coming out of the experiences that fill our day. For example, would we have been able to see parishioners who are marginalized, employees who are victimized, or hear the cry of children who are abused if our imaginations had not been formed by the new images of ourselves formed by the stories of Jesus? We respond the way we do because the images through which we see and interpret ourselves and what is going on around us make certain ways of acting appropriate or not. As we see the presence of God in more and more places of our life, we take on new ways of acting and bring a new tone and quality to our already habitual ways of acting. Part of the process of moral conversion is to refashion our imaginations with the images of Jesus and of ourselves and others so that we will live in ways that are harmonious with his spirit.

But catching the rhyme of biblical images and appropriate moral actions does not come naturally. As Spohn explains, it takes training, experience, a virtuous character, and a commitment to the way of life of discipleship. This helps explain why people can draw different conclusions about what is fitting from the same story. We differ morally not only because we choose different objects but also because we simply don't see things the same way. Each of us brings to our reading of the biblical story a different set of experiences, feelings, sensitivity to virtue, and depth of commitment to a life of discipleship. This also helps to show how morality acts back upon our spirituality in a dialectical fashion. Just as the spiritual practice of praying with biblical stories and images can give rise to moral action, so moral living can influence our spirituality by attuning us to the kind of life that fits the images. Spohn shows that Dorothy Day, for example, could discern a call to offer hospitality to the poor because she brought to her reading of the Sermon on the Mount a converted and generous heart already in tune with the poor.[23]

Spohn cautions, however, that we ought not to conclude that we are guaranteed moral implications faithful to the story of Jesus by merely invoking a biblical image. A self-serving heart can distort the analogy. For example, discrimination against women based on texts from Genesis 2:18 and Ephesians 5:22–24 is a constant reminder of how we can distort the analogy. While the analogical imagination guides moral discernment, it does not monopolize it. There are other sources of moral information that interact to form our moral judgment, such as an accurate knowledge of the situation, the tradition of theological reflection, the teaching of the church, moral principles, the witness of the faithful, and the rest of scripture.[24]

Eucharist Worship

In the first chapter, I tried to show that the moral life is, at its roots, an act of worship. That is, one's moral responsibilities are not merely to oneself and to others but also to God, present and active in the world. In the context of this chapter's interest in practices, we want to examine the relationship of liturgical worship in the Eucharist to morality. What is it about gathering as a community to read the stories of God and to share the same food at a common table that can make a difference in the moral life?[25]

One way of conceiving the relationship of worship and morality is to make morality extrinsic to worship. In this way of thinking, being moral is something we need to do so that we become worthy of worship. So, for example, we avoid sin in order to receive communion. Alternately, we might see morality as something that derives from worship as a sacramental effect. That is, we might think that we have become better persons because Christ now lives in us after we have said our prayers and received communion. The way of thinking represented in this chapter, however, maintains that morality is internal to the ritual actions that make up worship. To appreciate this internal link, we must remember that morality is not simply a matter of conforming to a set of rules. It is more the matter of orienting one's sensibilities and shaping one's perspective on the world. This way of appreciating morality puts worship more squarely in line with those influences on the formation of character, especially the imagination and dispositions of virtue, than it does with something extrinsic to right action.

Above all, worship is an act of loving God. We gather for worship primarily to give thanks and praise to God for what God has done and continues to do for us in the Spirit of the risen Lord. We do not gather in worship in order to derive moral imperatives or to become better persons. But by gathering in faith, we put ourselves in the presence of God's Spirit and allow God to make a claim on us through ritual actions such as gathering as a community, breaking open the word, and sharing the one bread and the one cup at a common table. These ritual actions link us to morality by having a formative influence on our identity, perspective, and dispositions.

The influence on identity comes from letting God have a claim on us in worship. Through worship, we define ourselves in relation to God and commit ourselves to what God cares about. Our religious identity can then serve as a critical alternative to any other relationship we might have or attachments we might acquire in the course of living out our responsibilities.

The influence on our perspective comes by participating in ritual actions filled with images that have the power to illumine the meaning and direction of our lives. While the Eucharist is the giving of praise and thanks to God, it simultaneously trains us how to see from the point of view of God. Through the Eucharist, God enters our world and we enter God's. The stories of scripture, the prayers of the liturgy, and the actions of the community inform our imaginations to give us a vision of what life looks like under God's rule.

Remember, an important part of the moral life is to see rightly, and seeing is an exercise of the imagination. Worship is the primary school for a religious imagination. Paul Wadell answers the title question of his article, "What do all those Masses do for us?" by saying that they form us into persons with a new vision that opens us to the attitudes and virtues of Jesus.[26] The eucharistic imagination envisions a community of forgiveness, mutual respect, and self-giving love. Participating in the Eucharist can play a role in shaping the way we envision life and our role in it because the images we find in the gathering community, proclaiming the word, and sharing the food can become our interpretive framework for discerning the meaning and direction of our lives.

What we enact ritually around the table of the Eucharist is the way we ought to live when away from the table. Take, for example, the symbolic actions of the community—diverse in age, race, gender, culture, and sexual orientation—gathering to confess their sins, to hear the word of God proclaimed, to profess a common faith, to pray a common prayer, and to share in the same food around the common table. Doing these actions together can help an individual worshiper identify with the vision and values of the community reflected in the Eucharist and hear the call to build an inclusive social order. As we have been welcomed and forgiven in the Eucharist, so we are to be hospitable and liberating in like manner. We who are reconciled to God and to one another around the eucharistic table are to be instruments of reconciliation, breaking down barriers that alienate and marginalize so that no one gets left out. This is how the moral life is informed by eucharistic spirituality.

Worship not only shapes the way we see the world, but it also affects the way we are disposed to act in certain ways toward the world. To say we love God in worship but not be disposed to the moral practice of loving and serving others is to misunderstand what makes for authentic worship. As we read in the First Letter of John, anyone who claims to love God but hates the neighbor is a liar (1 John 4:20–21). We cannot pretend to be relating to God whom we cannot see if we refuse to deal with our neighbors whom we can see. Worship schools the imagination and links us to virtue.

The Eucharist is to be a paradigm of a shared and sharing life. Participating in the Eucharist fosters participating in a communal life of interdependence marked by the virtue of solidarity among all. Solidarity is not a vague feeling of compassion at the misfortunes of others but rather a firm determination to commit oneself to promote the conditions necessary so that the good of all will flourish. Unfortunately, such a link between liturgy and justice was not a prominent feature of popular liturgical piety that marked the church in the decades immediately preceding the Second Vatican Council. Our eucharistic imagination then was too individualistic, and our practice of eucharistic worship too private. The Mass, by and large, provided a communal context for our private prayers. We gathered as a community and shared a common food, but too often we turned that action into a private moment to develop our relationship with Jesus and missed its social dimension calling for a commitment to justice.

Oscar Hijuelos depicts this very kind of spirituality in his character, Edward Ives, in the novel, *Mr. Ives' Christmas*. Edward Ives came of age in the 1940s. He prayed regularly, attended Mass faithfully, and instilled a love for prayer in his children. After the murder of his son, Ives's commitment to prayer did not falter even though he no longer felt the protection and love of God that he once knew. God seemed absent. But he still prayed persistently for forgiveness and reconciliation with the murderer. For decades Ives continued to go to Mass, where he prayed his own prayers. This was typical of the liturgical spirituality of that era. There is no hint in the novel that Ives ever saw that the prayers and ritual actions of the Mass could open him to the world outside himself. Eventually, Ives does experience the forgiveness, understanding, and redemption he long sought. But the Mass remained the communal context for his private meditation. For him, liturgical participation did not foster a grasp of the solidarity of the community that called him to set relationships right. He found it in other ways.

Separating liturgy from solidarity and its call to justice is not new. Saint Paul criticized the church in Corinth for profaning the Lord's Supper by not attending to the needs of others (1 Cor 11:17–34). The prophets of old spoke out against religious ritual unrelated to moral commitment. The prophets reminded Israel that worship is empty without social responsibility (Amos

5:21–24; Isa1:10–17;58). The prophet Micah asks about the kind of liturgy God desires. The answer is a formula for a way of life: to do justice, to love kindness, and to walk humbly with God (Mic 6:8). The test of our worship is in the quality of our commitment to justice, and not by what each gets out of it for private benefit.

Participating in worship can and ought to foster a sense of solidarity with those with whom we worship and for whom we pray, even if we don't know them personally. Since solidarity is not limited to caring only for friends or family, the Eucharist can school us in solidarity by providing experiences where bonds of affection with others have a chance to grow. That is, the Eucharist can express praise and thanks to God while it also engages people in sharing. We see this happening as we engage the multicultural nature of the church by celebrating each other's special festivals (Guadalupe, Saint Patrick's, Tet). Suburban parishes can partner with the less-well-off urban or mission parishes to share resources. Ecumenical projects can bring various religious traditions together around a common cause. Holy Spirit Parish/Newman Hall at the University of California in Berkeley announces each week the social agency that will receive a percentage of the week's collection. These are all ways to foster solidarity in a worshiping community so that the "Amen" we proclaim when receiving the Body of Christ in communion becomes a commitment to live in a life-giving way with the whole body of Christ.

Not every liturgy effectively influences the moral life. It is easy to participate in song, gesture, and action and still walk away untouched by what we are doing. There are many explanations for this. We don't always worship well. For some, excessive clericalism, exclusive language in our ritual prayers, readings, and preaching, and the exclusion of women from primary roles in worship are obstacles to letting the liturgy take us up into its life. For others, it may be the lack of clear symbols that connect the liturgy to life. Then there is the fact that we are all subject to the cultural blindness of individualism that prevents us from seeing the social commitment entailed in worship. The moral influence of the liturgy requires more than participation. It also requires the experience of a living community struggling to witness in life what it proclaims in its rituals.

Another explanation for the failure of the liturgy to influence the moral life has to do with competing images held out by the church and culture. This takes us back to the role of the imagination in our anthropology and to the important sources of influence on the imagination. As we saw with the film, *Life Is Beautiful*, Giosue is able to live with hope in a universe of death because the images his father created for him commanded more attention in his life than did the images of despair from the prison camp. Giosue's identification with his father was stronger than his identification with the culture of the camp. So his imagination was shaped more by the playful images of his father's games than by the brutal life of the prison.

When it comes to competing images of church and culture, the church simply does not command the full attention of many of those who come to pray. Because the liturgy is formed by the story of Israel and Jesus, its power forms us in its image and according to its sensibilities. But the moral imagination and sensibilities of many people are being shaped less by the Christian story and more by the media, self-help manuals, or the workplace. It is not the images and symbols of life and human relationships from our biblical stories and liturgical actions that dominate most people's imaginations, but the images of social interaction in sitcoms, consumer ads, police dramas, and professional sports that have the real mass appeal. Rituals and symbols train us to see, and so many of us have embraced cultural rituals, symbols, and celebrations as more expressive of who we are.

Take for instance the experience of Ann and Andy. At the ten o'clock Mass they hear the biblical word calling us to be mindful of the needs of others and to work toward a peaceful resolution of conflict in our social relationships. These are powerful images of self-giving and peacemaking heard in the context of a community marked by diversity. After Mass, Ann and Andy head for the sports bar where they meet their friends from work. For the next three hours they are immersed in images that promote aggressive competition as the primary mode of social interaction. The emotions, camaraderie, and rituals of the sports bar eclipse the biblical images for social interaction until they fade into insignificance. Ann's and Andy's story is not unique.

The stories and symbols that Ann and Andy live by, along with many people like them, are often not those of the Christian scriptures and our liturgical life. They may go to church on Sunday, but a thoroughgoing commitment to the vision of God, self, and others celebrated there is beyond their imagining and aspiring. They are more strongly attached to the practices and symbols of other centers of influence. While entering into the ritual process of the Eucharist enables us to confirm our religious identity, inform our imaginations so as to shape a new perspective, and to take on new dispositions toward virtue, there is no guarantee that it will happen. Mere formalistic participation is not enough. There must be soulful participation that both opens the imagination to the images that fill our worship and moves the heart. Only then will we embrace the relationships with God and with others that we acknowledge with our "Yes" to the word proclaimed and to the Body of Christ received.

Conclusion

Spiritual practices like prayer, biblical meditations, and eucharistic worship are our ways of responding to God's offer of love in and through which we draw closer to God and to one another. These practices are a focused opportunity to be addressed by God and a visible way to respond to God in the Spirit and to our belonging to one another in the body of Christ. When engaged with the right intention, spiritual practices have the power to transform our imagination and our moral sensibilities so that our experience of being loved can give rise to moral practices that will extend the range of love's influence in the world. This gets to the heart of spirituality informing the moral life and the moral life acting back upon our spirituality.

This interaction of spirituality and the moral life is the inner dynamic of the good life, the life in the Spirit to which we now turn.

6.

Life in the Spirit

❖

So far, we have seen that the Christian moral life is rooted in Christian spirituality and expresses it. Spirituality and morality must be closely related and must mutually influence one another because they share a common source and goal—experience of God's love and union with God. From the Christian perspective, who we become and how we behave derive from our relationship to God revealed in Jesus and kept alive in the Spirit. While we have reflected throughout this book on what it means to live in the Spirit, three aspects of the moral life, nurtured and sustained by spiritual practices, especially express the Christian moral life as a life in the Spirit. These are conversion, discipleship, and discernment. As a journey toward our fulfillment in God, everyday life requires ongoing conversion; growth in the Spirit of God implies sharing ever more completely in the paschal mystery of Christ as a disciple; and, the desire to live our commitment to follow Christ as a disciple under the guidance of the Spirit requires ongoing discernment. This closing chapter will sketch these three aspects as a summary of how our moral life embodies our spirituality.

Conversion

Conversion can be a troublesome notion for many of us. For one thing, conversion means change. After we have spent so much time trying to get our lives together, who wants to face the call to change? Conversion meets with resistance for other reasons, too. For instance, for some people conversion suggests a "Come to Jesus" revival meeting with its characteristic religious commotion—voices, visions, and demonstrations of emotion. If this is conversion, those who prefer a more subdued approach to religion want no part in it. For others, conversion is more properly applied to large-scale sinners, not to ordinary folks. For still others, conversion simply means changing churches (from Methodist to Catholic) or religions (from Judaism to Christianity).

Whatever the source of resistance to conversion, we cannot ignore its central place in the teaching of Jesus. "The time is fulfilled, and the kingdom of God has come near; repent, and believe in the good news" (Mark 1:15). The Gospel of Mark begins the public ministry of Jesus with this summary of his preaching. What, then, is the conversion to which we are called who have heard the preaching of Jesus and want to live a life in the Spirit?

Shuv is the Old Testament word for conversion. It suggests physically changing one's direction, that is, turning away from or turning back to someone. Its more spiritual sense is akin to our notion of an "attitude adjustment," a change of heart. This turning is more than simply changing one's mind or feeling differently. *Shuv* implies that the whole person turns back to God.

Metanoia is the New Testament word for conversion. It suggests an internal change that shows itself in one's conduct. While *metanoia* carries the basic meaning "to turn around," it does not refer exclusively to the radical about-face of those who had been standing in complete opposition to God. Conversion, as a call of the gospel, is for everyone, not just the notorious sinner who had made a radical choice for evil and selfishness as a way of life. Moreover, it is not a once-only turning. Conversion is an ongoing process of centering one's heart on God.

In the language of virtue ethics, the ongoing conversion to which one is called involves a change of heart and will that reaches into the depths of one's identity, since conversion engages all aspects of one's character. To be converted means to see in a new way, to think new thoughts, to hold to new convictions, to adjust one's attitudes and feelings, to form new relationships, to set new priorities in our values, and to do new deeds because we have encountered the transforming love of God. All of this is only possible because God loves us and we are free to cooperate with God's love. Conversion is not a self-made achievement, something we can make happen by following the strategies of the latest self-help seminar. Conversion is the invitation, support, and challenge of amazing grace.

Just as "blindness" is a good metaphor for sin, so "seeing" is a good metaphor for conversion. The shorthand description of conversion is captured in the familiar hymn, "Amazing Grace": "I once was lost, but now am found, was blind but now I see." In the New Testament, the most impressive and memorable story of conversion as a movement from blindness to sight is that of

Paul.[1] Its threefold repetition in Acts is enough to secure its importance (Acts 9:1–19; 22:6–16; 26:12–18). Paul, the zealous persecutor of Christians, finds his eyes opened to a new work, the work of the Lord whom he had been persecuting. Paul's conversion teaches us that turning to God in conversion is a response to God's love breaking into our lives to open our eyes and to change our hearts. Without an openness to love, we live in the dark, blinded by our own selfishness. When our hearts are open to love, we can see more clearly the life-giving, other-directed dimensions of all our relationships.

As with Paul, so with us: Conversion continues for a lifetime. It is not concluded in a moment. The critical moments of awakening are but a part of the larger process of re-imagining one's self and all of life. Lillian Hellman gives a marvelous image for understanding our lives as ongoing conversion in her description of "pentimento," which she uses to begin her book, *Pentimento: A Book of Portraits*:

> Old paint on canvas, as it ages, sometimes becomes transparent. When that happens it is possible, in some pictures, to see the original lines: a tree will show through a woman's dress, a child makes way for a dog, a large boat is no longer on an open sea. That is called pentimento because a painter "repented," changed his mind. Perhaps it would be as well to say that the old conception, replaced by a later choice, is a way of seeing and then seeing again.[2]

A life of ongoing conversion is like that. It is the matter of having old conceptions replaced by new images. Conversion does not forget the past by erasing it, but it reworks the past with a fresh understanding. Ongoing conversion proceeds by the yielding of one image to another, like the painting and repainting of a canvas according to the changing perspective of the artist. Openness to ongoing conversion keeps our lives from getting stuck in worn-out images of ourselves, others, and the world that no longer bear fruit.

Lillian Hellman underscores two important aspects of pentimento that are integral to ongoing conversion. First, replacing the old conceptions by later images is a matter of seeing, and then seeing again. There is freedom and growth here. It requires a deliberate choice of the will to alter an earlier image that no longer fits the new perspective of the artist. There is a sense of moving on, of acquiring a new perspective and seeing freshly. The old is reworked, not scrapped. The result is a new masterpiece. And so, too, with a life of ongoing conversion.

Second, in looking back over her life, Lillian Hellman rediscovers the meaning of her life by integrating the people and experiences that have made up her life into a new perspective. She lets go of what is no longer life giving and makes room for something new. Conversion is the willed process of reforming the imagination with fresh images of who we are, of what is happening to us, and of what is yet possible for us and our world. Life in the Spirit could not go on without these new images and the heartfelt desire to recreate our personal relationships and the whole of social reality in light of them.

Hellman's image of pentimento helps us to appreciate that the Gospels' call to conversion takes root in the imagination and shows itself in the deliberate desire to live differently. From the point of view of the imagination, conversion is a matter of re-imagining so as to see dimensions of reality that were not available to us before. The cry of Bartimaeus, "Let me see again" (Mark 10:51), is the cry of any person serious about the spiritual life and becoming a disciple. The world we live in is dictated by how we see it. If we change our perception, we change how we experience the world. In the moral life, remember, we respond to what we see. The great enemy of right living is not necessarily limited to a weak will; it could also be an impaired vision. Before we can answer the question, "What should I do?" we need to ask, "What is going on?" This is a matter of seeing. Deliberation and will follow to sharpen our perception and to focus our attention on a course of action.

Since what counts for us spiritually and morally depends a great deal on what we see, the ongoing process of conversion is necessarily rooted in our imaginations. As we imagine, so we act. Jesus used images and parables to convert the imaginations, and thus the lives, of his listeners. His new twist to homey examples in his parables, for example, got people to see in a new way that God's reign of love was in their midst and it called for a new way of behaving. In our own day, every teacher knows the power of an apt example, and every preacher knows the effect of a story well told. Those who listen but do not get the point do not lack intelligence. They are simply looking in the wrong direction. An example or story allows the listener to let a new image play on prior experience. Suddenly all is clear: "Oh, I get the picture! I've just never seen it that way before!" When we "get the picture," we have come upon an image that helps us put all the diverse parts together so that we can understand and respond appropriately. What we decide to do becomes a function of the "picture" we have of the world. When religious images, like blind Bartimaeus, a call to follow, the cross, "turning the other cheek," the Good Samaritan, the prodigal son, Mary's "Yes," are part of the imaginative process, they enter into the content of what we experience, and they contribute toward shaping our behavior according to the emotional content and the values entailed by those images. In the process of ongoing conversion to life in the Spirit, the images of life under the reign of God become our moral resources for challenging, correcting, or affirming, as the case warrants, the images we acquire from other worlds of influence on our lives.

Sometimes we just can't see clearly on our own. We need a guide. We are like the blind woman on a street corner in this story from John Shea:

> On a busy corner near where I live, a blind woman could not go forward. Her seeing eye dog had steered her up against a bus-stop bench and continued to nudge her against it. Every time she tried to push ahead, she just pushed against the bench. Finally, she called out, "Is there anybody there who can see." A man instantly and explosively responded, "I can, sister, I can." He helped her.[3]

Like this woman on the street corner, and like Paul, we need someone who can see better than we can. Having someone in our lives who can see when we are blind is one of the blessings of belonging to a community and to a tradition. Just as Paul had Ananaias, we too have the help of another, like a spiritual director, a pastoral counselor, a preacher, or just a good friend who can help us notice and make the connection between the mystery of God and what is happening to us. Part of the ministry of the word in the church is to give us eyes to see the signs of divine love stirring in the ordinariness of our lives. When we see through the images of Christian beliefs, we do not abandon the data of the senses, but we do change the way we see them: what looks like a victim is our neighbor; what appears to be an achievement is pure gift; what feels like a coincidence is grace; what seems to be insignificant is pure gold. Learning to see is what spiritual disciplines, like praying with the scripture, and what spiritual guides help us to do.

Conversion, then, is fundamental to living in the Spirit. It is the gift from God that opens our eyes to the presence of the Spirit at work in our midst; and it leads us to respond to all things in their relation to God. Such a way of responding expresses our faith in Jesus Christ alive in the Spirit and our commitment to become disciples continuing the mission of Jesus under the same Spirit.

Discipleship

At the heart of Jesus' moral message is the radical call to leave all things and "then come, follow me" (Matt 19:21). The same grace that calls us to conversion is the grace that supports our following Jesus as a disciple.

Given the differences of historical and social context between the time of Jesus and our own, discipleship cannot mean simply accepting literally every command of Jesus, nor can it mean reproducing the externals of his life and work as if we were invited to an exercise of nostalgia. Just as we would not want to say that following Jesus as a disciple today means that we have to be carpenters, Jewish, males, and itinerant preachers, so we do not want to say that we must die at the hands of political and religious leaders because Jesus did, or that we are free to relate to others without regard for appropriate boundaries because Jesus was not afraid to touch or to be touched by people like lepers, sinners, children, or women. Trying to transpose everything that Jesus did into our own day is anachronistic and reductive. It commits us to mimicry and even misplaced and inappropriate behaviors. Mimicry is the death of faithful, creative discipleship.

Authentic imitation is living by analogy in the spirit of Jesus. It is having "the mind of Christ" (1 Cor 2:16), that is, having the dispositions and values of Jesus so that we can be creatively responsive to the needs of our day in the ways that harmonize with the way of life exemplified in him. The challenge of discipleship is to make Jesus' way of life our own, not by duplicating it point for point, but by living in his spirit and by means of the Spirit. The question of discipleship for us is not "What would Jesus do?" Although well intentioned, that question too easily opens the way to fundamentalistic mimicry. The challenging question for us is "How can we be as faithful to God in our day as Jesus was in his?" Of course, we cannot deduce faithful behavior from a particular command or deed of Jesus by strict logic. However, we can use the stories of Jesus as our primary examples of fidelity; we can discover what is fitting in our new situation by moving analogically from his story to the demands of our own life to discover how our character and actions might harmonize with his. The discussion from chapter 5 on praying with scripture and the analogical imagination pertain by way of suggesting how to create that harmony.

The spiritual roots of Jesus' ministry were in his "Abba" experience of divine love. The secret of his living a life of self-offering love is his feeling secure in the Father's love. The Gospel accounts of his baptism in the Jordan convey how Jesus must have experienced himself as someone special in God's eyes: "This is my Son, the Beloved, with whom I am well pleased" (Matt 3:17; Mark 1:11; Luke 3:22). The rest of the Gospel demonstrates the practical effect of his holding fast to these words of worth received out of the waters of baptism. Jesus lived out of a heart that treasured God. As the Gospels have it, when our hearts treasure God, all other treasures will be treasured rightly (Matt 6:21; Luke 13:34). Jesus lived with his heart set on doing what he understood the Father to be asking of him. In being so faithful, he lived free of false loves so that he could embrace the whole world in an inclusive love just as he understood the Father to be doing. As disciples, we are to do likewise.

Because Jesus knew whose he was, he did not have to latch onto false loves in order to secure his identity. Discipleship begins with letting go. By following the way of renunciation (Mark 8:34), we can rest secure in God's loving us. So we have to let go of the attachments and illusions that enslave us, such as our desire for recognition to secure our identity, our attachment to position, power, or prestige to secure our worth, or our reliance on obeying the laws or saying our prayers to save us. Unless we give up the presumption that we can insure our lives by creating these surrogate loves, we are not ready for discipleship. To be a disciple demands the freedom to let go of our self-made securities that occupy our hearts so that we have room for divine love. Secured in divine love, we are called to the same freedom and faithfulness that Jesus knew.

While Jesus did not leave a detailed program of action that we are to follow as disciples, he did leave his vision of the reign of God and the commission to proclaim it in word and witness. The focus of his ministry was the reign of God. He saw the reign of divine love as embracing all humanity and honoring the basic equality of each person without the limitations of nationality, race, or religion. Within his vision of God's reign is the point of reference for discipleship—inclusive love.

Inclusive love is the characteristic that distinguishes Jesus from other religious personalities or established groups of his time. For example, Jesus did not exclude sinners from his company, as did the Pharisees. Even prostitutes and tax collectors, the most notorious of sinners, were welcome at his table. Salvation for Jesus did not mean condemning sinners from afar, but going forth to meet them and offer them a way out of their sin by building new relationships. Nor did Jesus exclude the crippled, the infirm, the possessed, or the unclean, as did the Essenes; nor did he exclude the poor and needy as did the wealthy Sadducees. Jesus had no fear of approaching these sorts of people, for it was the Father's love for them that motivated him to touch and heal them. Jesus also rose above the narrow nationalism of the Zealots, who restricted their mission to Israel. Jesus was faithful to the Father, and not just to the God of the Jews. While the society of his time regarded women and children as defenseless property, Jesus did not exclude women from his company of intimate friends or children from his presence. But he championed them as witnesses to the reign of God. In the imitation of his Father's love that transcends all forms of particularism and exclusivism, Jesus made inclusiveness the basic value for anyone who would be identified with him and his mission.[4] In this way, Jesus showed concretely what life in the Spirit looks like. From him we learn that the criterion for discipleship is to be able to make room in one's heart for everyone, and especially to be ready to stand on the side of those who are the weakest and lowliest in society.

Jesus modeled what taking this stand for inclusive love would look like in the way he interpreted the meaning and use of power. His use of power stands in complete contrast with the way officials of society and religion at that time were conceiving and exercising it. Jesus did not distrust power as such, but he conceived it as mediating divine love through service that liberates and unites, and not as a force that dominates and devours the vulnerable (cf. Mark 10:29–42; Matt 20:25–28; Luke 22:25–27). Jesus' singular devotion was to do the Father's work of setting people free and inviting all into communion with God and with one another. His miracles, for example, are great works of liberation. His parables are often judgments on the use of power to exclude. Jesus was free enough to include and serve a great variety of people despite features that made many of them outcasts to their own people. To be converted as a disciple is to become committed to the same liberation to which Jesus was committed.

That this was such a new teaching for his disciples is evident in how they and the religious leaders of that time often served as foils to Jesus' loving use of power. Consider, for example, the conflict between Jesus and his disciples who return to him after meeting a man casting out demons in Jesus' name (Mark 9:38–40; Luke 9:49–50). The disciples want to stop this man. Why? He is not one of their company. Jesus, however, does not want to stop him. "Whoever is not against us is for us," says Jesus. The disciples want to use their power to control the good and to make themselves superior to another who is not one of them. The fact that a man now lives free of demons is insignificant to them. What matters is that *they* did not work the wonder. The power directed by divine love does not want to usurp the good; the arrogant power that seeks to remain superior does.[5]

We can also see this liberating power at work in the scene of healing the bent-over woman in Luke 13:10–17. In this scene Jesus calls to a woman who has been bent over by an evil spirit for eighteen years. He places his hands on her, and she stands up straight. She who was once weak is now strong. Friends of Jesus rejoice over her liberation, but the officials of the synagogue who observe this are angry over what was done and when it was done. The power that liberates by making the weak strong is too challenging to the community. Arrogant power of superiority wants to control the good by keeping some weak while others remain strong. The power that Jesus expresses is the power that transforms the structures of domination in the community.[6]

The great reversal of structures of power that Jesus reveals is especially evident in the famous conflict between Jesus and Peter in the foot-washing scene in the Gospel of John (John 13:6–10). When Peter sees Jesus, the master, acting like the servant, he knows that something is wrong. It is not the picture he has in his imagination of the structure of power in the community. So Peter resists being washed. He realizes that if he complies with this washing, he would be accepting a radical reversal of the very structures of domination upon which he depends for his power. Such a conversion, both in his imagination and in his life, is more than he is willing to undergo. When Jesus deliberately reverses social positions by becoming the servant, he witnesses to a new order of human relationships in the community whereby the desire to dominate and establish superiority has no place. Power in the disciple is not for domination but for service.[7]

The passion story ultimately brings the issue of power to a climax. In Gethsemane, Jesus' opponents come with familiar instruments of the power that guarantees domination: betrayal, arrest, swords, and clubs. Jesus has no such weapons. Those who hold positions of superiority according to the social structure of that day, Sanhedrin and Roman procurator, abuse him. Roman soldiers torture him with the very symbols of superiority—a purple robe, a crown (of thorns), and homage (of spittle and blows). The ultimate weapon of the power of domination is public execution on the cross. In the crucifixion, the power of domination is raging out of control.

Yet the very success of this power is its own subversion. In dying on the cross, Jesus does not resort to legions of angels to destroy the evil of those who appear to be in power. If he did, then his kind of power and theirs would be the same. The only difference would be in the size of the muscle. Jesus resorts to the only kind of power he knows—divine love—and offers forgiveness. The cross ultimately reveals the emptiness of oppressive power that devours the weak.[8] The passion and death of Jesus reveal the steadfast love of God unmasking the arrogance of power that nailed him up. That same steadfast love invites disciples of all ages to live as Jesus did—trusting in the power of divine love to sustain us.

The life of Jesus shows us that all those things that we think are necessary to guarantee our love and loveableness really count for nothing. The cross witnesses to that. The cross stands as the central symbol of the disciple's life not because it is a symbol of self-sacrifice, but because it is the summary of the freedom and faithfulness that marked Jesus' life. Up to the cross, Jesus emptied himself of all he could give. On the cross, he is most empty of what he could do for himself. The resurrection affirms that the way of Jesus is a truthful expression of life under the reign of God. Where Jesus has gone, we are bound to follow if we catch his spirit and follow his example. If we are to be disciples in the spirit of Jesus, then we must be free enough to nurture in ourselves moral sensitivities that have a special concern for those who are hurt or lost, that make room for the stranger and the outcast, that are disposed to act toward others with mercy and forgiveness, and that are inclusive of all. Because of the resurrection, we can take the risk to love as Jesus did. The love that characterizes the disciples witnessing to the reign of God is the inclusive love of those who have learned to live as friends and not to fear each other.

But we cannot become disciples on our own. Just as conversion required a community, so does discipleship. We learn discipleship by being initiated into it by others. To imitate Jesus requires that we first become part of a community pledged to be faithful to him. Unless we establish strong bonds of solidarity with others who share in the vision and mission of Jesus, we will not be able to remain committed to discipleship.

Even within a community of disciples, many of us may feel that the call to be free and faithful in the way of Jesus is far out of reach. The words of Mother Emmanuel, head of the Carmelite monastery in Mark Salzman's novel *Lying Awake*, could be words addressed to us: "No matter how many times we hear what it costs to follow Christ, we're still shocked when the bill comes, and we wonder all over again if we can pay it."[9] This seemingly unattainable life of a disciple only reminds us that we are all works in progress. We are always letting go and learning to love with a more inclusive love. The call to discipleship invites us to go beyond where we are now, to open ourselves to divine love, and to live as friends. Each of us will live as a disciple in a way that corresponds to our openness to the Holy Spirit. Jesus has shown us the way of inclusive love and liberating power. But the details will be of our own making. The form we give to our discipleship will fit the circumstances, needs, and problems of our day in a way that witnesses to the vision of Jesus: that all peoples be brought under the inclusive reign of divine love. To respond in the spirit of Jesus to the diverse situations that face us requires a capacity for discernment so that we will express our moral character in a way fitting the call of discipleship and the demands of our situation.

Discernment

The challenging question of discipleship—"How can we be as faithful to God in our day as Jesus was in his?"—connects our believing in Jesus and the Spirit with behaving in a way that harmonizes with the spirit of Jesus. Discernment is our bridge between believing and behaving.

In the narrow sense, discernment is the matter of having a fine sense of discrimination between degrees of importance. The ability to discern requires keen perception, sensitivity, and imagination. As an aspect of life in the Spirit, discernment is the capacity for testing the "spirits," or the "movements of the heart," to detect which ones reflect the God-prompted desires of the human spirit. To be out of touch with these desires is to be out of touch with the action of the Holy Spirit in our lives, for it is through desire that the human spirit touches the Holy Spirit, who gives us a sense that we are moving toward or away from God. Discernment treats these inner movements of affection, often called "consolation" and "desolation," as surer guides to the deepest truth about ourselves than are the thoughts or ideas going on in our heads. The goal of discernment is to keep our lives in line with the drift of our deepest desire for God. The discerning judgment is more like the artist's aesthetic judgment that something is fitting than the referee's judgment that a play is in bounds. Discernment is a clear example of spirituality and morality working together for it reaches into the heart wherein lie our fundamental experience of God and commitment to God.

As people of faith, we believe that moral living involves more than the occasional solving of problems. Rather, the moral life is the daily graced response to the presence and action of God in our lives. Discernment is the habit of discovering the most fitting ways to express what our relationship to God demands from us. But the process of discernment is not like using a vending machine from which, if we follow all the steps, we will get what we want. While there are some indispensable elements and principles of discernment, these do not do the work. The degree of clarity in hearing God's invitation depends a great deal on how well tuned our ears are to the call of God. William Spohn offers this illuminating analogy to express what is required:

> A piano tuner ought to know how to read music, strike the keys on the keyboard, work the pedals, and be able to tighten or loosen the piano strings to produce true notes. None of these skills will help if she does not have a good ear for pitch. The criterion for tuning pianos is internal. Only a very accurate sense of pitch will tell whether the notes being sounded are true or off. The skill lies in registering harmony so acutely that the slightest deviation is detected.[10]

Analogously, discernment requires an "ear" for God, or a keen religious sense that has internalized the "mind of Christ." This makes discernment an art and a science; it is both affective and rational at the same time. It requires the capacity for distinguishing and discriminating between possible courses of right actions by drawing not only on principles but also, and more crucially, on intuition, emotion, and somatic reactions that give us a fine feeling for what our relationship with God as disciples today ought to be like.

Discernment takes us beyond simply doing the right thing to doing what is most fitting. It wants to find the way that is consistent with our fundamental commitment to God in this set of circumstances. Does this action fit whom we want to become as disciples of Jesus for today? Discernment looks for the right thing to do in light of our most fundamental relationship in life—our commitment to God. Discovering the call of God in our life is more than disciplined deliberation. It is the graced exercise of faith seeking to express itself in action.

To develop the art of discernment requires a degree of faith and personality development that would enable us to have a sufficient grasp of how God acts in our lives and of who we are. If we do not yet have faith so as to be open to the presence of God in the depth of human experience, or if we lack sufficient self-possession so as to be able to give direction to our lives, or if we are not sufficiently stable emotionally so that we are able to live with a certain degree of uncertainty, or if we are not yet free enough to care about others and commit ourselves to the well-being of others, then we are not ready to discern. In this case, we ought to follow reliable rules, the advice of a trusted friend, or someone in authority.

THE CALL TO HOLINESS

The process of discernment discovers what we are called to do by putting the head and heart in dialogue. When we embark on the road of discernment, we commit ourselves to a process that, like a four-stranded cable, circles back upon itself to inter-twine faith, reason, emotion, and intuition.[11] Faith gives us a per-spective and context for interpreting what is going on and for setting priorities. Reason helps us assess further the scope of our moral experience and study the multiple relationships of the factors that make it up. Emotions are those inner feelings that give us our first evaluation of what is going on, and intuitions give us an immediate grasp of the responsibilities we have in the situation before we become consciously aware of them through reason.

When we say that we are "wrestling with a problem," "mulling it over," or "praying about it," we mean that we are seeking the harmony of these four strands by engaging the back-and-forth movement of head and heart. The harmony of these strands is confirmed by the experience of interior balance and peace, which gives us the confidence that this is what God is calling us to do. Finding the path that harmonizes with our basic orientation to God is what discernment seeks. There are some principles behind it:

1. *Character is crucial.* Character represents our persistent beliefs, ideals, values, attitudes, and perspective that serve as the point of reference against which we judge what we ought to do. We feel most comfortable with what fits the kind of person we are and so naturally choose that path. Since we generally stay "in character," our moral life has a momentum toward a well-established way of judging and acting. That is what makes

character so crucial for discernment. It gives us what the moral tradition has called a "connatural" knowledge for what fits our fundamental disposition. We saw this asset at work in the Good Samaritan nurse from chapter 3. Someone who is disposed to be compassionate, as she is, will spot the comforting thing to do without being instructed to do it. The honest person spots deception quickly; the manipulative person finds ways to be deceptive without any effort.

While character is crucial, not just any type of character will do for discerning life in the Spirit. Since discernment seeks to find that course of acting that harmonizes with our character, having a character fundamentally oriented toward God and what God cares about is important if we are to live in the Spirit. Such a character is our way of cooperating with God's Spirit and acquiring the spirit of Jesus. The more we have this built-in "homing device" for God, the more likely we are to discern the call of God in the situation.

2. *The whole network of human ways of knowing must be engaged.* Our discernment will be as reliable as the extent to which we know the territory of our experience both outside and inside ourselves. Getting to know the territory outside ourselves engages the conscious mind and its powers to gather data, to order it, and to make rational sense of it. But discernment also engages the unconscious, the affective, intuitive, and somatic ways of knowing. In fact, the unconscious and the body respond to our experiences more quickly and sensitively than does our rational analysis. We know in our dreams and in our bodies before we know in our minds what way of life fits our character

and commitment. Physical symptoms of distress and chronic discomfort are often clear signs that we are going against our own truth. A body that is in harmony is often a reliable sign that what we are doing is right for us.

Our emotions and intuitions give us an initial interpretation of our experience before we begin to reflect on it. Emotions and intuitions alert us to subtle nuances in the situation that the disinterested, detached reason can miss. They also help us recognize the particular and personal response that fits us in this situation. But we need to be critical of our emotions and intuitions, too. While they can communicate their own insights, they can also perpetuate their own prejudices. While we need to trust them for the personal dimensions of experience they open to us, we need to distrust them for their potential to mislead us. A sound moral discernment is never purely an emotional or intuitive conclusion; but neither is it purely cognitive. The critical mind and the reasoning heart must work together to inform and check each other. To follow the process of discernment of spirits adequately, then, we need to engage all of the ways of knowing.

3. *The imagination is our window on the world.* All that we said in chapter 3 about the imagination comes into play in the process of discernment. What we decide to do is greatly influenced by what we see going on and by what we envision as possible. Through the imagination we can walk around inside the world of our anticipated choices to see what life feels like inside each option. Without the imagination we would not be able to recognize the complex web of responsibilities in a particular case, to entertain options, or to anticipate consequences.

4. *Prayer is the context for discernment.* Since discernment is the process of interpreting the affective movements evoked by our experiences and by imaginatively engaging our options, it requires some "downtime" for us to become aware of these movements. So that they can present themselves with God's support, this downtime must be spent in the context of faith. Prayer provides that space. The prayer of discernment is an attitude of openness to God's presence and a willingness to listen so that we can hear the call of God through all the voices and noise in our life. Moreover, prayerful openness to what is going on inside us and around us is a way to free ourselves from external pressures and selfish preferences that fix our hearts in advance on one particular way of responding.

Prayerful listening seeks the interior freedom that leaves us open to God's call. Achieving this freedom is not easy. There are so many attachments or illusions that want to enslave our hearts, such as our fear of change, peer pressure, status, and the need for control. The regular rhythm of prayerful listening, along with good physical and emotional health, and sometimes the guidance of a wise helper may be the key to unlocking our imaginations and letting go of those paralyzing attachments that prevent us from hearing God's call. We cannot hear God's invitation if we are caught up in hectic activity or subject to physical distress, chaotic emotions, or mood swings that obscure or confuse God's call to us coming through our internal and external experiences.

5. *Clarity does not guarantee certainty.* In the process of discernment the head and heart are working together. We gather

data and put it into logical relationships so that we can draw a tentative conclusion. We also process data intuitively and emotionally to give us a hunch of where the data is directing us. But the subjective factors attended to in prayer and the objective factors attended to in gathering our evidence do not add up in a neat logical sum to a clear, unambiguous conclusion. Each of our sources of wisdom weighs in, but no one monopolizes to settle the matter. Faith, reason, emotion, intuition work together until a specific direction emerges. While only a system of tight syllogisms that leaves no room for the affective and intuitive can guarantee logical certitude, the process of discernment seeks the option that "rings true" inside us at a level deeper than what our head tells us is reasonable. That is why we can say that discernment does not give us the logical certainty of a syllogism but rather the moral certainty of converging probabilities in a well-tuned heart. In discernment, a probable conclusion is the best we can hope for, since there will always be variables we overlook or don't anticipate. We must always recognize the limits of the process and make only modest claims that we know what God is asking of us now.

6. *By their fruits you will know them.* In the image of Saint Paul (Rom 8:16), the Holy Spirit joins with the human spirit at the level of our deepest desires. We confirm our contact with the Holy Spirit not by the criteria of strict logic, but by the aesthetic criterion of a deep feeling of inner peace and harmony. We can say that our decision fits us when it "rings true" to who we are, and when we feel good about ourselves when we are living out the decision. Or, in a contemporary idiom, we feel that we are "in flow" so much so that we may even lose track of time and our

surroundings. The feeling that something fits us, or that we are "in flow," will be judged ultimately by whether it delights us and brings a sense of wholeness. But sometimes we mistake the relief we feel after struggling to make a decision with the peace, delight, and harmony of discernment. Since we can easily be deceived, we need to watch for signs of confirmation that our decision truly is leading us to union with God.

The internal signs of confirmation are the affective experiences of confirmation and desolation. Consolation is the experience of harmony that shows itself in those experiences described as fruits of the Spirit in Galatians 5:22 — "love, joy, peace, patience, kindness, generosity, faithfulness, gentleness, and self-control." The experience of consolation does not mean that all ambiguity is gone and that everything will be rosy from then on. The consolations tell us that we are moving toward greater personal wholeness and are cooperating with the work of the Holy Spirit in our lives. Consolation is confirmed by the passion we have for what we are choosing and the energy we get from pursuing it. Desolation, on the other hand, tells us that we are resisting the Spirit. In desolation, gloominess replaces gladness, confusion replaces peace, coldness replaces warmth, aridity replaces passion, boredom replaces energy, and we tend to lose confidence in God's love for us. To get out of desolation, we explore the sources that brought us to that condition and then engage in activities that enhance the direction of our lives taken when experiencing consolation.

The external signs of confirmation are the fruits of greater love (Matt 7:15–21). When we are cooperating with the Spirit, we are free enough to enhance the quality of life and love among those with whom we live and work. We do not need to live in fierce competition with anyone but can accept our limits, rejoice in the gifts of another, and receive them as complementary to our own. Another external sign is the confirmation by the community that our giftedness is responding to what the community needs. But we must proceed with caution in applying this criterion, since some of us are called to stand against the community as its prophets. In this case, what ultimately leads to greater love and unity may at first create division. Only time will test the quality of the person's love for the community.

Discernment puts us in touch with our movements toward or away from God. While it does not give us the certitude we might want to have in giving direction to our lives, it does nurture our desire to live more consciously and freely in the service of God. The movement toward God finds its external expression in the steady desire to love God and to love our neighbor as ourselves. This is where spirituality and the moral life mutually influence and inform one another.

Conclusion

Spirituality and the moral life are ultimately about life in the Spirit. It all begins with God loving us and calling us into being. Now the whole of our life is a response to this love we have received as pure gift, amazing grace. We have Christ as our model to show us the way to live with this gift, and we have the Spirit alive in our hearts and in the community of believers to make it possible.

Spirituality and morality are necessarily closely related because they have a common origin and endpoint—the experience of God and union with God. Since God is ever present to us in the Spirit at the depths of human experience, we really cannot clearly separate our relationship to God (spirituality) from the way we live in the world (morality), for our relationship to God is mediated by the way we respond to all things. Though not clearly separated, they can be distinguished on the basis of their primary concerns. Spirituality focuses on our relationship with God and morality on who we are to be and how we are to behave in the world. For the Christian believer, who we are and how we behave are functions of our experience of God. Our moral life flows from and is informed by our spirituality, and our spirituality is, in turn, shaped by our moral life. Spirituality and the moral life are about living in this world with a sense of belonging to God, of being loved by God without condition, and of being invaded by the presence of God everywhere. To try to live with God in all that we do is to become holy. To strive to love in the imitation of God is to become a good person. When our striving to be holy and our efforts to be good mutually inform each other, then we have found a life of friendship with God lived through loving one another in the imitation of Christ and under the power of the Spirit. We call that living the good life.

Notes

❖

Chapter 1: What Are We Talking About?:

1. See the account of his life in "St. Simeon the Stylite," *Butler's Lives of the Saints*, vol. 1, ed. Herbert Thurston and Donald Attwater (New York: P. J. Kenedy & Sons, 1956), 34–37.

2. Nikos Kazantzakis, *Zorba the Greek*, trans. Carl Wildman (New York: Simon and Schuster, 1952).

3. Lawrence S. Cunningham and Keith J. Egan, *Christian Spirituality: Themes from the Tradition* (New York: Paulist Press, 1996), 22–28.

4. This description of spirituality is highly influenced by the work of Sandra Schneiders and her appeal to a broadly based approach to spirituality. See especially, "Theology and Spirituality: Strangers, Rivals, or Partners?" *Horizons* 13 (Fall 1986): 266, and "Spirituality and the Academy," *Theological Studies* 50 (December 1989): 684.

5. Schneiders, "Theology and Spirituality," 267.

6. The relational-responsibility model of morality is often associated with H. Richard Niebuhr, *The Responsible Self* (New York: Harper & Row, 1963); Bernard Haring, *Free and Faithful in Christ*, vol. 1, *General Moral Theology* (New York: Seabury Press, 1978), and

Notes

Charles E. Curran, *The Catholic Moral Tradition Today: A Synthesis* (Washington: Georgetown University Press, 1999).

7. For a well-developed argument on the love of God at the foundations of the moral life, see Edward C. Vacek, *Love, Human and Divine: The Heart of Christian Ethics* (Washington: Georgetown University Press, 1994).

8. Edward C. Vacek, "Love for God—Is It Obligatory?" *Annual of the Society of Christian Ethics* (1996): 220.

9. For Keenan's argument, see his "Proposing Cardinal Virtues," *Theological Studies* 56 (December 1995): 709–29.

10. William C. Spohn, *Go and Do Likewise: Jesus and Ethics* (New York: Continuum, 1999), 157.

11. On habituation as critical practice in Aristotle, see Nancy Sherman, *The Fabric of Character: Aristotle's Theory of Virtue* (Oxford: Clarendon Press, 1989), 176–83.

Chapter 2: Where Have We Been?

1. See Sandra Schneiders, "Scripture and Spirituality," in Bernard McGinn and John Meyendorff, eds., *Christian Spirituality: Origins to the Twelfth Century*, vol. 16 of *World Spirituality: An Encyclopedic History of the Religious Quest* (New York: Crossroad, 1986), 10–15.

2. John Mahoney, *The Making of Moral Theology* (Oxford: Clarendon Press, 1987), 1.

3. John T. McNeill, *The Celtic Churches: A History* A.D. *200 to 1200* (Chicago: University of Chicago Press, 1974), 84.

4. John T. McNeill and Helena M. Gamer, *Medieval Handbooks of Penance* (New York: Octagon Books, 1965), 88.

5. Ibid., 99.

6. Ibid., 92–93.

7. Ibid., 46.

8. Kilian McDonnell, "The Summae Confessorum on the Integrity of Confession as Prolegomena for Luther and Trent," *Theological Studies* 54 (September 1993): 423.

9. John A. Gallagher, *Time Past, Time Future: A Historical Study of Catholic Moral Theology* (New York: Paulist Press, 1990), 18–20.

10. McDonnell, "Summae Confessorum," 423.

11. Philip Sheldrake, *Spirituality and History: Questions of Interpretation and Method* (New York: Crossroad, 1992), 41–44.

12. Ibid., 44.

13. Yves M-J Congar, *A History of Theology*, trans. and ed. Hunter Guthrie (Garden City: Doubleday, 1968), 166.

14. Thomas Slater, *A Manual of Moral Theology*, vol. 1 (New York: Benziger Brothers, 1908), 5–6.

15. Ibid., 6.

16. John C. Ford and Gerald Kelly, *Contemporary Moral Theology*, vol. 1, *Questions in Fundamental Moral Theology* (Westminster: Newman Press, 1958), 97–98.

17. Henry Davis, *Moral and Pastoral Theology* (London: Sheed & Ward, 1941), I, 3–4.

18. Ibid., 2.

19. Pierre Pourrat, *Christian Spirituality: From the Time of Our Lord till the Dawn of the Middle Ages*, trans. W. H. Mitchell and S. P. Jacques (New York: P. J. Kenedy and Sons, 1922), v.

20. Adolphe Tanquerey, *The Spiritual Life*, 2nd rev. ed., trans. Herman Branderis (Tournai: Desclee & Co., 1930), 5.

21. Joseph de Guibert, *The Theology of the Spiritual Life*, trans. Paul Barrett (New York: Sheed & Ward, 1953), see 6–7.

22. Louis Bouyer, *The Spirituality of the New Testament and the Fathers*, trans. Mary Perkins Ryan (New York: Desclee, 1960), see

viii–ix; see also *Introduction to Spirituality*, trans. Mary Perkins Ryan (New York: Desclee, 1961).

23. Ford and Kelly, *Contemporary Moral Theology*, vol. 1, 99.

24. See James F. Keenan, "Ethics and Spirituality: Historical Distinctions and Contemporary Challenges," *Listening* 34 (Fall 1999): 170. See also Jordan Aumann, *Christian Spirituality in the Catholic Tradition* (San Francisco: Ignatius Press, 1985), 144–217.

25. Mahoney, *Making of Moral Theology*, 29.

26. Michael Downey, *Understanding Christian Spirituality* (New York: Paulist Press, 1997), 61–62.

27. Gallagher, *Time Past, Time Future*, 29.

28. Downey, *Understanding Christian Spirituality*, 58–59.

29. Mahoney, *Making of Moral Theology*, 27–36.

30. Downey, *Understanding Christian Spirituality*, 75–84.

31. Emile Mersch, *Morale et Corps Mystique* (Paris: Desclee de Brouwer, 1937). *Morality and the Mystical Body*, trans. Daniel F. Ryan (New York: P. J. Kenedy & Sons, 1939).

32. Gerard Gilleman, *The Primacy of Charity in Moral Theology*, French ed. (Paris: Desclee de Brouwer et Cie, 1952), trans. from the 2nd French ed. William F. Ryan and Andre Vachon (Westminster: Newman Press, 1959).

33. Fritz Tillman, *The Master Calls*, trans. Gregory J. Roettger (Baltimore: Helicon Press, 1960).

34. Bernard Haring, *The Law of Christ*, 3 vols., trans. Edwin G. Kaiser (Paramus: Newman Press, 1961–1966).

Chapter 3: Being Human Before God

1. For an accessible view of what a biblically based anthropology can contribute to spirituality, see Michael D. Guinan, *Human Before*

God: Insights from Biblical Spirituality (Collegeville: Liturgical Press, 1994).

2. On the use of these anthropological terms as synecdoche, see John W. Cooper, *Body, Soul, and Life Everlasting,* rev. ed. (Grand Rapids: William B. Eerdmans, 2000), 44.

3. See the discussion of *ruah* in Hans Walter Wolff, *Anthropology of the Old Testament* (Philadelphia: Fortress Press, 1974), 32–39.

4. Gerald G. May, *Addiction and Grace* (San Francisco: Harper & Row, 1988).

5. For situating the fundamental option within Karl Rahner's anthropology, see Rahner, *Foundations of Christian Faith,* trans. William V. Dych (New York: Seabury Press, 1978), 90–106. For an extended theological discussion of fundamental option in light of Karl Rahner and Pope John Paul II's encyclical on moral theology, *Veritatis Splendor* (1993), see the papers of the Karl Rahner Society of the CTSA in 1996 published in *Philosophy & Theology,* vol. 10, no. 1.

6. Bernard Haring, *Free and Faithful in Christ,* vol. 1, *General Moral Theology* (New York: Seabury Press, 1978), 189–93.

7. See especially Thomas Moore, *Care of the Soul* (New York: HarperCollins, 1992).

8. Wolff, *Anthropology of the Old Testament,* 18.

9. Ibid., 40.

10. Ibid., 40–55. On the "heart" as an aspect of biblical anthropology, see also Heinz-Josef Fabry, *"Leb,"* in *Theological Dictionary of the Old Testament,* ed. G. Johannes Botterweck, Helmer Ringgren, Heinz-Josef Fabry, trans. David E. Green, vol. VII (Grand Rapids: William B. Eerdmans, 1995), 399–437; see esp. 412–34.

11. Wolff, *Anthropology of the Old Testament,* 51. Wolff notes that "heart" occurs more frequently in the Wisdom literature than in any other place. See 47.

Notes

12. John Shea, *Starlight* (New York: Crossroad, 1992), 102–3.

13. Ibid., 103.

14. See M. Shaughnessy, *Feelings and Emotions in Christian Living* (New York: Alba House, 1988).

15. Daniel C. Maguire has contributed significantly to understanding the affective or mystical dimension of morality. See especially his *The Moral Choice* (Garden City: Doubleday, 1978), 71–75, 84–86, 263–67, 281–305.

16. More attention is being given today to the role of feelings in the moral life. In addition to the work of Daniel C. Maguire cited in n.15, see also G. Simon Harak, *Virtuous Passions* (New York: Paulist Press, 1993); Timothy O'Connell, *Making Disciples* (New York: Crossroad, 1998), 65–74; Russell B. Connors, Jr., and Patrick T. McCormick, *Character, Choices and Community* (New York: Paulist Press, 1998), 189–94; and William C. Spohn, *Go and Do Likewise: Jesus and Ethics* (New York: Continuum, 1999), 120–41; Justin Oakley, *Morality and the Emotions* (New York: Routledge, 1992). From the point of view of psychologists interested in ethics, see Charles Shelton, *Morality of the Heart: A Psychology of the Christian Moral Life* (New York: Crossroad, 1990) and his *Achieving Moral Health* (New York: Crossroad, 2000); also see Sidney Callahan, *In Good Conscience* (New York: HarperCollins, 1991), 95–113.

17. Callahan, *In Good Conscience*, 95–113; Shelton, *Achieving Moral Health*, 58–61.

18. O'Connell, *Making Disciples*, 70–73.

19. Callahan, *In Good Conscience*, 106–9, and Shelton, *Achieving Moral Health*, 59.

20. On emotional and moral perception, see Nancy Sherman, *The Fabric of Character: Aristotle's Theory of Virtue* (Oxford: Clarendon Press, 1989), 44–50.

21. Paul Ricoeur, *Fallible Man*, trans. Charles Kelbley (Chicago: Henry Regnery Company, 1967), 200.

22. Maguire, *Moral Choice*, 282; Callahan, *In Good Conscience*, 99–106; Shelton, *Achieving Moral Health*, 59.

23. See, for example, Karl Rahner, *The Dynamic Element in the Church* (New York: Herder and Herder, 1964), 161ff.; Daniel C. Maguire, "The Knowing Heart and the Intellectualistic Fallacy," in *The Moral Revolution* (San Francisco: Harper & Row, 1986), 259–61; Andrew Tallon, "The Heart in Rahner's Philosophy of Mysticism," *Theological Studies* 53 (December 1992): 711.

24. Joseph Allegretti, "A Person of Character," *Health Progress* 71 (April 1990): 88.

25. For a review of this research, see Callahan, *In Good Conscience*, 186–90. See also Shelton, *Morality of the Heart*, 33–59, and *Achieving Moral Health*, 124–39.

26. Sidney Callahan, "The Role of Emotion in Ethical Decisionmaking," *Hastings Center Report* 18 (June/July 1988): 14.

27. Shea, *Starlight*, 103–4.

28. Robert Bolt, *A Man for All Seasons* (New York: Vintage Books, 1960), 81.

29. See, for example, L.A. Hart, *Human Brain and Human Learning* (New York: Langman, 1983), 41. On the use of this science in the realm of faith, see David L. Loomis, "Imagination and Faith Development," *Religious Education* 83 (Spring 1988): 251.

30. Two helpful sources for understanding the imagination in spirituality and morality are Kathleen R. Fischer, *The Inner Rainbow: The Imagination in Christian Life* (New York: Paulist Press, 1983), and Philip S. Keane, *Christian Ethics and the Imagination* (New York: Paulist Press, 1984).

31. Robert N. Bellah, et al., *Habits of the Heart: Individualism*

Notes

and Commitment in American Life (Berkeley: University of California Press, 1985).

32. See, for example, William F. Fore, *Television and Religion: The Shaping of Faith, Values, and Culture* (Minneapolis: Augsburg, 1987).

33. James M. Gustafson, *Can Ethics Be Christian?* (Chicago: University of Chicago Press, 1975), 65.

34. J. Philip Newell, *Echo of the Soul* (Harrisburg: Morehouse Publishing, 2000), xi–xii.

35. See N. P. Bratsiotes, *"Basar," Theological Dictionary of the Old Testament,* ed. G. Johannes Botterweck and Helmer Renggren, trans. John T. Willis, vol. II (Grand Rapids: William B. Eerdmans, 1975), 317–32, see esp. 328.

36. Ibid., 325–26. See also John W. Cooper, *Body, Soul, and Life Everlasting,* rev. ed. (Grand Rapids: William B. Eerdmans, 2000), 40–41.

37. On the body in Pauline theology, see Joseph A. Fitzmyer, "Pauline Theology," *The New Jerome Biblical Commentary,* ed. Raymond E. Brown, Joseph A. Fitzmyer, and Roland E. Murphy (Englewood Cliffs: Prentice Hall, 1990), 1406, 1409–10.

38. On the place of the body in rationality and the scientific evidence to support it, see G. Simon Harak, *Virtuous Passions* (New York: Paulist Press, 1993), 7–26.

39. James B. Nelson has done some of the most creative work on the relationship of sexuality and spirituality. See especially *Embodiment* (Minneapolis: Augsburg, 1978); *Between Two Gardens* (New York: Pilgrim Press, 1983); and *Body Theology* (Louisville: Westminster/John Knox Press, 1992).

40. Michael Downey, *Understanding Christian Spirituality* (New York: Paulist Press, 1997), 45.

41. This theme has been developed at great length by liberation theologians; see esp. Jon Sobrino, *Spirituality of Liberation: Toward Political Holiness* (Maryknoll: Orbis, 1988).

42. This harmonizing is what biblical scholars call "stereometric thinking." For a discussion of this kind of thinking, see Wolff, *Anthropology of the Old Testament*, 7–8.

43. For a summary discussion of key aspects of Rahner's anthropology, see Karl Rahner, *Foundations of Christian Faith*, 24–43.

Chapter 4: Experiencing God

1. Mary Doria Russell, *The Sparrow* (New York: Fawcett Columbine, 1996), 100.

2. Oscar Hijuelos, *Mr. Ives' Christmas* (New York: HarperCollins, 1995), 101.

3. Ibid., 102.

4. Helen Keller, *The Story of My Life* (New York: Grosset & Dunlap, 1902), 23–24.

5. Russell, *Sparrow*, 401.

6. Pat Collins, *Prayer in Practice* (Maryknoll: Orbis, 2001), 88–89.

7. John Shea, *Starlight* (New York: Crossroad, 1993), 83.

8. Paul Tillich, *The Shaking of the Foundations* (New York: Scribners, 1948), 57.

9. Karl Rahner, "The Experience of God Today," *Theological Investigations*, trans. David Bourke, vol. XI (New York: Seabury Press, 1974), 154.

10. Karl Rahner, *Do You Believe in God?* trans. Henry J. Koren (New York: Paulist Press, 1971), 4–5. See also Rahner, "Experience of the Holy Spirit," *Theological Investigations*, trans. Edward Quinn, vol. XVIII (New York: Crossroad, 1983), 200–203.

Notes

11. Mark Salzman, *Lying Awake* (New York: Alfred A. Knopf, 2000).

12. Patricia Livingston, *This Blessed Mess* (Notre Dame: Sorin Books, 2000), 65.

13. Robert Wuthnow, *Creative Spirituality* (Berkeley: University of California Press, 2001), 262–63.

14. Anne Lamott, *Traveling Mercies* (New York: Anchor Books, 1999), 117.

15. For an excellent introduction to the importance of images and the imagination in spirituality, see Kathleen R. Fischer, *The Inner Rainbow: The Imagination in Christian Life* (New York: Paulist Press, 1983); for a major work on the imagination in the moral life, see Philip S. Keane, *Christian Ethics and Imagination* (New York: Paulist Press, 1984).

16. Hijuelos, *Mr. Ives' Christmas*, 92.

17. Ibid., 93.

18. James M. Gustafson, *Can Ethics Be Christian?* (Chicago: University of Chicago Press, 1975), 87–114.

19. For an extensive treatment on the doctrine of the Trinity and its practical dimensions, see Catherine Mowry LaCugna, *God for Us: The Trinity and Christian Life* (New York: HarperCollins, 1991).

20. Michael J. Himes and Kenneth R. Himes, *The Fullness of Faith* (New York: Paulist Press, 1993), see esp. 55–63.

21. Elizabeth A. Johnson, *She Who Is: The Mystery of God in Feminist Theological Discourse* (New York: Crossroad, 1992).

22. Alice Walker, *The Color Purple* (New York: Washington Square Press, 1982); for this whole scene, see 175–79.

23. Ann Carr, *Transforming Grace* (San Francisco: Harper & Row, 1988), 135–39. Johnson, *She Who Is*, 33–41.

24. Sandra Schneiders, *Women and the Word* (New York: Paulist Press, 1986), 41.

25. Ibid., 30.

26. Ibid., 47.

27. Julian of Norwich, *Revelation of Love*, trans. and ed. John Skinner (New York: Doubleday, 1996), chap. 58, p. 130.

28. Sallie McFague, *Models of God* (Philadelphia: Fortress Press, 1988), see esp. part 2, pp. 91–180.

29. Karl Rahner, "The Spirituality of the Church of the Future," *Theological Investigations*, vol. XX: *Concern for the Church*, trans. Edward Quinn (New York: Crossroad, 1981), 149.

Chapter 5: Practices: Spiritual and Moral

1. Alasdair MacIntyre introduced the notion of "practices" into ethics in *After Virtue* (Notre Dame: University of Notre Dame Press, 1981). See also Maria Antonaccio, "Contemporary Forms of *Askesis* and the Return of Spiritual Exercises," *Annual of the Society of Christian Ethics* (1988): 69–92. Among theologians, see Margaret R. Miles, *Practicing Christianity* (New York: Crossroad, 1988), and Dorothy C. Bass, ed., *Practicing Our Faith* (San Francisco: Jossey-Bass, 1998). Among ethicists, see William C. Spohn, *Go and Do Likewise: Jesus and Ethics* (New York: Continuum, 1999), and the work ed. by Nancey Murphy, Brad J. Kallenberg, and Mark Thiessen Nation, *Virtues and Practices in the Christian Tradition* (Harrisburg: Trinity Press International, 1997), and also Martha Ellen Stortz, "Practicing Christians: Prayer as Formation," in *The Promise of Lutheran Ethics*, ed. Karen L. Bloomquist and John R. Stumme (Minneapolis: Fortress Press, 1998), 55–73. Among social scientists, see esp. Robert Wuthnow, *After Heaven: Spirituality in America Since the 1950s* (Berkeley: University of California Press, 1998).

Notes

2. Wuthnow, *After Heaven*.

3. On the devotional manuals and their connection to the practices that shape the religious self, see Miles, *Practicing Christianity*.

4. On the "role of rote" and practices as "embodied rote," see Timothy E. O'Connell, *Making Disciples* (New York: Crossroad, 1998), 148–50.

5. As recounted in Spohn, *Go and Do Likewise*, 48.

6. Ibid., 14.

7. Wuthnow, *After Heaven*, 185.

8. Robert Wuthnow, *Creative Spirituality* (Berkeley: University of California Press, 2001), 130.

9. Wuthnow, *After Heaven*, 194.

10. Wuthnow, *Creative Spirituality*, 138.

11. There are many fine books on prayer available today. Two recent ones of special interest to the theme of this chapter are Pat Collins, *Prayer in Practice* (Maryknoll: Orbis, 2000), and William A. Barry, *With an Everlasting Love* (Mahwah: Paulist Press, 1999).

12. Sebastian Moore, *The Fire and the Rose Are One* (New York: Seabury Press, 1980), 11.

13. John Shea, *An Experience Named Spirit* (Chicago: Thomas More Press, 1983), 153.

14. Anne Tyler, *Saint Maybe* (New York: Ivy Books, 1991).

15. On prayer of petition as an expression of absolute surrender to God, see Karl Rahner, *Christian at the Crossroads*, trans. V. Green (New York: Seabury Press, 1975), 48–61; see esp. 55–59; also, see Rahner and Karl-Heinz Weger, *Our Christian Faith*, trans. Francis McDonagh (New York: Crossroad, 1981), 51–69.

16. Dietrich Bonhoeffer, *Life Together*, in *Dietrich Bonhoeffer Works*, vol. 5, ed. Geffrey B. Kelly and trans. Daniel W. Bloesch and James H. Burtness (Minneapolis: Fortress Press, 1996), 90.

17. *Ibid.*

18. For a brief description of the ways *lectio divina* can be understood, see Lawrence S. Cunningham and Keith J. Egan, *Christian Spirituality* (New York: Paulist Press, 1996), 38–40.

19. For a succinct treatment of this form of prayer, see David Lonsdale, *Eyes to See, Ears to Hear: An Introduction to Ignatian Spirituality* (London: Darton, Longman and Todd, 2000), 110–25.

20. O'Connell, *Making Disciples*, 68.

21. Spohn, *Go and Do Likewise*, 50–71.

22. The significance of vision in the moral life has been a consistent theme in the writing of Stanley Hauerwas. He set forth this theme in his early essay, "The Significance of Vision: Toward an Aesthetic Ethic," in his collection *Vision and Virtue* (Notre Dame: Fides Publishers, 1974), 30–47.

23. Spohn, *Go and Do Likewise*, 65.

24. Ibid., 63, 69–71.

25. The interest in the relation of liturgy and the moral life has been given serious attention by both ethicists and liturgists. See the early collection of essays on this topic in *The Journal of Religious Ethics* 7 (Fall 1979). There was a reprise on this issue twenty years later in a special seminar at the gathering of the Society of Christian Ethics. For these articles, see *The Annual of the Society of Christian Ethics* (1999). Don Saliers has been a significant voice exploring the relation of liturgy and ethics. See the collection of essays done in his honor, along with his own response, in *Liturgy and the Moral Self*, ed. E. Byron Anderson and Bruce T. Morrill (Collegeville: Liturgical Press, 1998). On the relation of liturgy and justice, see the collection ed. by Kathleen Hughes and Mark R. Francis, *Living No Longer for Ourselves* (Collegeville: Liturgical Press, 1991).

26. Paul J. Wadell, "What Do All Those Masses Do for Us?" in Hughes and Francis, eds., *Living No Longer for Ourselves*, 153–69.

Chapter 6: Life in the Spirit

1. On this interpretation of Paul's conversion, see Ronald D. Witherup, *Conversion in the New Testament* (Collegeville: Liturgical Press, 1994), 65–68.

2. Lillian Hellman, *Pentimento: A Book of Portraits* (Boston: Little, Brown & Co., 1973), 3.

3. John Shea, *Starlight* (New York: Crossroad, 1993), 73.

4. On this characteristic of the inclusiveness of Jesus in contrast to the other religious personalities and established groups of his day, see Hugo Echegaray, *The Practice of Jesus*, trans. Matthew J. O'Connell (Maryknoll: Orbis, 1984), chap. 3, pp. 39–67.

5. For this interpretation of the liberating power in the ministry of Jesus, see John Shea, "Jesus' Response to God as Abba: Prayer and Service," in *Contemporary Spirituality: Responding to the Divine Initiative*, ed. Francis A. Eigo (Villanova: Villanova University Press, 1983), 54.

6. For this interpretation, see Mary Daniel Turner, "Woman and Power," *The Way Supplement* 53 (Summer 1985): 113–14.

7. For this interpretation of the foot washing scene, see Sandra Schneiders, "The Foot Washing (John 13:1–20): An Experiment in Hermeneutics," *Catholic Biblical Quarterly* 43 (January 1981): 76–92; see esp. 80–88.

8. For this interpretation of the passion from the perspective of power, see Donald Senior, "Passion and Resurrection in the Gospel of Mark," *Chicago Studies* 25 (April 1986): 21–34, esp. 25–27.

9. Mark Salzman, *Lying Awake* (New York: Alfred A. Knopf, 2000), 172.

10. William C. Spohn, *Go and Do Likewise: Jesus and Ethics* (New York: Continuum, 1999), 152–53.

11. This model is inspired by the work of Sidney Callahan, *In Good Conscience* (New York: HarperCollins, 1991). I developed this model at greater length in my book, *Moral Discernment* (New York: Paulist Press, 1997). It has a close affinity with the holistic understanding of conscience and the model of decision making found in Charles E. Curran, *The Catholic Moral Tradition Today: A Synthesis* (Washington: Georgetown University Press, 1999), 182–90.